'*The Sex Thing* is a much-needed challenge to any
A timely reminder of the need to intentionally
conversations about sex. With practical advice and examples, and building on
years of experience and insightful new research, Rachel helps unpack how we
can begin to have healthy conversations with our young people about sex, relationships and intimacy.'
Jimmy Dale, National Youth Evangelism Officer

'Rachel Gardner is a brilliant, courageous leader with decades of experience on
the frontlines of relational ministry. I'm so glad she has written this important,
insightful and ground-breaking book. *The Sex Thing* shows us how to put Jesus
at the centre of conversations about sex with empathy, understanding and grace.'
Pete Greig, 24-7 Prayer International and Emmaus Rd Church

'This book addresses one of the great blind spots of the church in our time. There
seems to be a great hunger amongst leaders and pastors to engage in conversations about spiritual formation, and simultaneously, a great reluctance to engage
in conversations about sexual formation. The silence is agony, particularly for the
next generation who are looking for guides to help them navigate this incredibly
complex cultural moment. We desperately need courageous voices to break the
silence ... Praise God, Rachel Gardner has broken the silence and exposed
the blind spot. When it comes to reimagining conversations with young people
about sex, I honestly can't think of anyone I'd rather sit at the feet of to learn.'
Pete Hughes, Lead Pastor at KXC

'This book is everything we need it to be and more. As a church leader and as
a mother of two preteens, I'm grateful for Rachel's honesty, wisdom and challenge for us to leave behind awkward mumblings [about sex] and instead have
informed, relevant and real conversations that are so much wider than sex talks
of the past. *The Sex Thing* overflows with beautiful theology, helping us to guide
our young people as they grow in their relationship with God and apply what
they know about who he is to their lives.'
Ali Martin, Soul Survivor Watford

'Probably the most important topic that the young people in your life are already
thinking about, hearing about and talking about. In this moment, where it's so
vitally important we shape those conversations and create safe spaces [where
young people] can make sense of the powerful messages they are bombarded
with, Rachel has written a fantastic book to guide, equip and provoke your own
thinking. Anyone who ever talks to teens should read this.'
Dr Kate Middleton, Psychologist and Director of The Mind and Soul Foundation

'Rachel is a gift to youth ministry: she is passionate, funny, enthusiastic, and always able to shake things up in a creative and unrestrained way. This book [feels] like you are in a conversation with Rachel about topics that young people long to explore. If you love young people and you want to be empowered to have conversations about sex, relationships, and all the stuff in between, then this is a must-read.'
Zeke Rink, Youth Network Associate Pastor, Vineyard Churches

'Over the last decade or so, no subject has felt more challenging - or more blurry - for Christian youth leaders to address than sex. In a culture that is moving so fast, the old principles for guiding young relationships suddenly feel like a poor fit, if indeed they ever did fit at all. The church has been crying out for someone to bring fresh vision, and a perspective that is both holistic and holy to this area… and now here it is. Rachel Gardner is the UK church›s trusted voice on sex and relationships and young people; many youth workers like me will feel incredibly grateful that she has chosen to write this vital book.'
Martin Saunders, Director, Satellites

'I'm praying this culture-changing book into the hands of every Christian parent and youth leader, in the hope that the honest conversations it encourages raise up a new generation of believers, sexually liberated by the gospel of Jesus.'
Ed Shaw, Ministry Director, <www.livingout.org>

'These are incredibly confusing and pressurized times for young people - and for youth leaders and parents. How do we navigate this new ever-changing sexual revolution in healthy and helpful ways? Rachel has written a book to help us, and it is utterly brilliant. It's thought through and thoughtful. Bold and brave. Honest and vulnerable. Powerful and practical. Packed with grace and truth bombs by the bucket load – by the skip load! And that's what we need as we approach this together with young people. We need to be people who are full of grace and truth. Discovering what is true and helpful and healthy really matters. But that journey of discovery only works if it's motivated by, and modelled in, unconditional love and grace. Rachel models this for us. She's got a track record. She's got her own story. She's not afraid to "go there". May her example, and what she's written in this stunning book, help us to "go there" too. There's too much at stake if we don't.'
Matt Summerfield, Senior Pastor, Zeo Church

Rachel Gardner has been working with young people, youth workers, church leaders and parents for more than two decades and has authored several books, including *The Girl De-Construction Project, Cherished* and *The Dating Dilemma*. She is the founder of the Romance Academy (featured in the BBC three-part documentary *No Sex Please, We're Teenagers*) and is President of the Girl's Brigade England and Wales. She is on team at Youthscape and co-leads a youth resourcing church in Blackburn, Lancashire, with her husband Jason. They have two children.

THE SEX THING

Reimagining conversations with young people about sex

Rachel Gardner

First published in Great Britain in 2021

Society for Promoting Christian Knowledge
36 Causton Street
London SW1P 4ST
www.spck.org.uk

British Library Cataloguing-in-Publication Data
A catalogue record for this book is available from the British Library

ISBN 978-0-281-08645-0
eBook ISBN 978-0-281-08646-7

Typeset by Manila Typesetting Company
First printed in Great Britain by Ashford Colour Press
Subsequently digitally printed in Great Britain

eBook by Manila Typesetting Company

Produced on paper from sustainable forests

To the brilliant, wild and devoted youth leaders I've had the joy of working with over the years:

Louise, Dan, Jo, Rachel, Woody, Katy, Segun, Lynne, Pete, Andrea, Helen, Jenni, Kelly, Mark, Rebecca, Sam, Mike, Joe, Beth and Jerome.

Contents

Contents

Introduction
The thing is

Isn't it funny how sex is often called 'it'?

'Have you done *it* yet?'

'At what age should I start talking about *it* to my kids?'

'Does God get angry if I do *it* with someone I'm not married to, even if I love them?'

Sex as a thing, something we cannot or don't want to give a name to. Even the word 'sex' is shorthand for something much broader that includes sexual behaviour, biological differences between male and female bodies, sexual thoughts and feelings, and reproduction. Scroll through social media or switch on Netflix and sex seems to be everywhere – knocked about, joked about, shocked about, aroused about but not properly *spoken* about. What about in church, our youth groups or families – how is sex reduced to an 'it' there?

My church doesn't talk about it, maybe they're scared we'll do it if we hear them say it!

I want to talk about it with my kids, I just don't know where to start.

If we talk about it in youth then we'll have to talk about porn, masturbation, being gay, virginity – that leaves me feeling out of my depth, to be honest.

Maybe, in choosing not to name sex, we think it can remain a thing that can be put somewhere. Contained. Explained in short sentences. Restrained by strict rules. But the thing is, whatever our reasons for not talking about sex, we need to. The way we talk about sex and hear sex talked about informs what we think about sex. And what we think about sex informs how we behave when it comes to sex. So 'it' matters.

What might happen if we were to talk about sex properly? Not in general terms but in specifics. What if we were to give names to the things we want to talk about? Things like love. Pleasure. Power. Porn. Attraction. Shame. Faithfulness. What if we were to call body parts by their real names? Parts like vagina, penis, breasts. And what if we were to talk about body-related things, like puberty, thrush infection, erectile dysfunction, orgasms? How might young people benefit if we, as youth workers, pastors, church leaders, parents, were prepared to reimagine bold, new conversations about sex – *all* of it? What information and encouragement might we need to stop us feeling ill-equipped and overwhelmed in our conversations with young people about sex?

I'm not quite sure when talking about sex with teenagers started for me. I was thinking about this the other day when a young person phoned to chat through a 'thing'. 'A phone sex thing,' she said. 'Is it OK for Christians to do? I don't know; it feels weird. But also, not. I'm still not sure what God thinks about it.'

I won't recount our conversation. Mainly because it's private. Also because I don't really remember what I said. It's not that I was uninterested in her conclusion – I've been discipling her for nearly a year and am deeply invested in seeing her grow and her love for Jesus grow. But my role in that phone call was to help her reach her own conclusion with her God-goggles on, to stretch out in her Christian faith identity. I was needed to listen with love and to amplify the wisdom she was vocalizing. I needed to bear witness to her awesome courage in being prepared to reflect on what an adolescent disciple of Jesus does about phone sex – a practice that *none* of her peers are asking ethical or moral questions about. I mean, how many adult Christians do you know who are asking theological, cultural, relationally reflective questions about phone sex? Exactly!

But for young disciples, finding their way at such a time as this, understanding what the gospel has to say about issues such as phone sex, is the tip of the iceberg. Thanks to the intersection of sexuality and rapidly advancing technology, the way young people are dating, falling in love and experiencing relational and sexual intimacy is radically changing. Emoji-themed vibrators, sex-capable artificial intelligence (AI) with

2

multiple personalities, limitless online sexual entertainment, Deepfake technologies,* the rise in techno-sexualities so people can live with life-sized dolls rather than other human beings: all these are not in some distant future; they're here now. We're also experiencing a radical shift in our understanding of an individual's sex and gender identity. Ideas that were self-evident a generation ago are under heavy strain as they are deconstructed at breathtaking speed.

This new immersive world of sexual expression and self-identification needs to be talked about. What it means to be a Christian teenager in this rapidly changing world needs to be talked about. And who better to lean in to these conversations among emerging generations of Jesus followers than people like you and me who, for all our brokenness and, at times, uncertainty, are clinging to Jesus and wanting him to take a front seat in this, one of the most important conversations of our age.

Changing conversations

I've spent the majority of my adult life talking with young people about sex.

The moment you take that out of context it looks odd, and I suppose in a way it is. It was never my intention to be known for talking about sex. I sort of fell into it. It was while studying theology at Bible college in the late 1990s that I began to be curious about how the gospel connected to the emerging narratives around post-modernity and third-wave feminism. I was intrigued by how young people were finding faith in an age of rapid deconstruction and acceleration into new norms.

These were the days before formal youth ministry qualifications, so after some short courses run by a local authority around supporting vulnerable young people, I took up a job working with the YWCA in the south of England. I began to notice how the young people I spent time with were really struggling to resolve those key identity questions: Who am I? Who likes me? Where do I belong? Arguably, since the invention of the 'teenager' (created by marketeers in the first place), young people have had these

---

* Deepfake technologies are AI-generated media that can seamlessly place anyone in the world into a photo or film they never actually appeared or participated in.

questions used against them to keep them consuming the latest products. But these were the early days of the digital revolution. Social media platforms were still embryonic ideas in Silicon Valley, but the disastrous impact of mass media's ability to skilfully sell perfection to young people desperate to know who they should be was already evident in young people's attitudes and behaviours. The fear of not ever being enough, but the compulsion to never stop trying to reach that goal, was already crushing a generation.

At that time, the focus of society's fears around adolescent sexuality was unplanned pregnancies. The UK had the highest rate of teen parents in the western world. In 1990, the number of under-16s giving birth had risen 10 per cent since 1981. The narrative in some quarters was accusatory: 'They only do it to get a flat.' Girls were shamed and boys weren't in the frame. In 1999, the Teenage Pregnancy Strategy for England was launched, with the aim of halving the rate of under-18 conceptions by 2010, from a baseline of 46.6 per 1,000 women. But it wasn't just pregnancy rates that were high. The rapid spread of sexually transmitted infections (STIs), particularly chlamydia and gonorrhoea, among sexually active young people was a serious cause for concern.

I was once asked by a head teacher to inform hundreds of suspicious-eyed teenagers seated before me in a secondary school assembly that empty crisp packets can't be used as condoms and having sex standing up doesn't prevent pregnancy. They didn't believe me. They didn't believe me the following year when I was back again to explain that 'blue waffle' was not a real STI resulting in death, but fake news.

The concept of sexual consent wasn't widely taught. If young people were receiving any sex education at secondary school, they were mostly learning how to put a condom on a courgette. I'm not belittling that; I hope there were young people who practised safer sex as a result. But the gaps in education and support were evident even then. When were young people being invited into healthy conversations about love, intimacy, manipulation, faithfulness, power, relationships, emotional safety? Where were the opportunities for them to explore and participate in trying out different approaches to their sexual well-being and relational health?

The 1990s were a bit of a glory time for church-based youth work. Many churches in the UK were still connecting with fairly large groups of young people. Drop-in youth clubs were successful, youth conferences and festivals were kicking off, school Christian-Union-type groups were thriving, and youth workers were running faith-based roadshows in schools around key Christian values. There was also a lot of momentum on the evangelical Christian scene around helping young people resist the pressures of youth culture. Fuelled by a desire to slow down young people's acceleration into the dangerous world of sexual exploration, books like *I Kissed Dating Goodbye* by Joshua Harris and movements like The Silver Ring Thing and True Love Waits were jumped upon by many Christian parents and leaders as magic bullets to protect their young people. They presented powerful codes of behaviour around dating, virginity, sex and the importance of chastity that quickly became ingrained in the normal narratives of church engagement with young people. In the UK, Steve Chalke's 'Don't touch what you haven't got' added to the zeal of sexual abstinence that was to shape for the next decade many churches' communication to young people about sex. But for all this interest in the sex lives of young people, I'm not sure how well we were engaging the young people themselves in their sexual development, let alone connecting that with a Christian faith identity. I know I wasn't.

Risk-averse

As a highly risk-averse, anxious, often socially awkward young woman, new to youth work and with very little confidence in dating relationships, I was trying on all the big purity practices for size. After a panicky weekend thinking I was pregnant after a kissing session with a boyfriend got especially heated (we both remained fully clothed) and a humiliating evening confessing to a church leader how bad I was for kissing a guy I'd just met at a bonfire, I opted to become SFJ (Single For Jesus). This bizarrely named label served as an effective blocking mechanism while I desperately tried to hold at bay awakening sexual thoughts and feelings. No one told me that I couldn't date, kiss or hold hands with boys, but as the girls who enjoyed kissing boys seemed to be a cause for concern, I ended up believing that everything other than an enthusiastic NO to anything remotely to do with sex or romance was displeasing to God. I internalized the behavioural codes of the community without really

5

knowing what was 'groupthink' and what was my own conviction. I received all disapproval as the conviction of the Holy Spirit – and I was racked with grief and shame. It made me quite hardline in my thinking and equally self-righteous in my attitude towards others.

I wince at some of my self-righteousness as a young Christian, but at the time I felt lost. I couldn't see my way through the mess of reality and was preoccupied with what it meant to be sold out, all *souled* out, to Jesus when I had a body whose needs and desires I couldn't predict or control. What did my shifting feelings of sexual attraction *mean*? And what was I meant to *do* with the things I thought and felt or wanted to experience? Even as these questions were raging inside, I was being drawn into increasingly complicated pastoral situations with the young people I met.

Lost

I remember visiting a sexual health clinic with two teenage girls. Their story was heartbreaking. One of them had 'lost my virginity and my tights' at a party the week before because she was 'sick of being the only girl in Year 10 who was still a virgin'. Can you imagine that pressure? Being the 'only one'?

'How did that feel, thinking you were the only virgin in your year?' I asked.

'Horrible. I didn't want to be that girl who hasn't had sex.'

'What could happen if you were that girl who hasn't had sex?' I asked.

'You get called frigid, by the boys and the girls. And all the other girls hate you.'

The conversation went on. All the while her best friend was silent. I was curious. Turning to her I asked, 'What do you think?'

'Don't ask her,' the first girl interrupted with a smile. 'She started having sex with her boyfriend last year!'

'I didn't,' she mumbled. 'I've not done it yet . . .'

'But you said . . .'

It was a devastating moment for these two friends. Huge decisions had been made on the basis of a story that wasn't true. I vowed in that moment to spend my life encouraging young people to ask questions, to challenge the status quo and to think for themselves so that they could act for themselves and *as* themselves: beloved, purposed, empowered, free human beings.

Then there was Toby and Jade, two young Christians, newly in love and tied up in knots about how to physically express that. Their relationship ricocheted between pleasure and guilt until one evening, after youth cell, they sat and sobbed out their confusion and shame. I sat, desperate to say something that could make sense of this for them, all the while wondering if it was at all possible to be faithful to a sexual ethic of celibacy outside marriage while retaining any sense that your sexual self is good.

The more I listened to young people, the more I saw that what would begin as a question about heartbreak or when to start dating would quickly move on to issues of profound self-worth and purpose. These embodied conversations with young people became the door into the holy, soulful place where the biggest questions of life were asked. It was like watching a bonfire being lit – tiny sparks igniting flames of curiosity to know the bigger things of life, to have their greatest 'why' questions answered. Sex chats led us to God chats, time after time after time.

Here and now

That was many years ago, in the days before Snapchat, WhatsApp, Twitter, Instagram, TikTok and online porn. Before the dip in teen pregnancy rates. Before society had fully woken up to the crisis in young people's mental health. Before groups like Fight the New Drug and Naked Truth were using an evidence-based approach to show how accessing online porn rewires the adolescent brain and recalibrates society's understanding of intimacy. Before the #MeToo movement. Before terms like CSE (child sexual exploitation) and FGM (female genital mutilation) meant anything to the average church youth worker. Before Josh Harris bravely apologized for writing books that unintentionally but seriously caused hurt through unbiblical demands on a generation of young disciples.

Youth culture has shifted and continues to move rapidly. The advancement in sex-tech and changing societal attitudes towards sexual behaviours and identities means we're preparing young people for a world we don't fully understand. In addition, decades of secularization and culture change has weakened youth engagement with the church, and vice versa, contributing to our nervousness to engage young people in our churches in conversations about sex. We're increasingly aware of the role the church has played historically in sidelining sexual minorities and shaming people for stepping outside a biblically historic view of sex, so many of us are united in our desire to avoid presenting a damaging narrative to an emerging generation who quite simply don't really get where the Church is coming from on these topics. If it's silencing our voice in young people's lives in our church communities, how much more ill-equipped are we feeling about engaging young people in the wider community? Might this be why leading Christian organizations like ACET UK are seeing fewer Christian participants on its Esteem sex and relationships training programmes? Has talking about sex just got less interesting for young people? I don't think so. Has talking about sex got more complicated for us as Christian leaders? Absolutely.

This has got me wondering what the Church needs to do in the next few years to form a sexual ethic that young people could thrive in. What shape would our conversations take? How might we become the compassionate enablers young people need us to be on their journey towards sexual maturity?

Why this book?

This book is my attempt to hold space to explore these conversations with grace, humility and conviction. My hope is that it will genuinely and generously resource and embolden you as you lean in to the lives of the young people you have been called to serve. Your ministry among young people is needed now more than ever before. This is the time to reimagine conversations about sex and to embrace the abundant space that opens up when young people feel safe enough to think, reflect and act boldly.

Part 1

Part 1 explores how the UK Church has engaged with young people on the topic of sexual identity and sexual practice. We'll consider how we've sometimes got these conversations right and sometimes got them wrong. Delving into a bit of adolescent identity formation, the process of puberty and teenage brain science, we consider how young people's sexual scripts (their ideas, values and behaviours) are shaped by both internal and external pressures. Knowing how young people's sense of self is shaped is vital in helping us engage with how they are reshaped in Christian discipleship. To this end I also explore the impact of purity teaching in the Church and ask what a sexual reformation of engaged holiness among Christian young people might look like. I would advise against skipping straight to Part 2 as we need to understand where we are and why before we can reimagine our conversations with young people about sex.

Each chapter ends with a section entitled 'Outside in; inside out', in recognition that as youth practitioners we are being influenced by a context (outside in) and constantly speaking into a context (inside out). The 'outside in' questions encourage you to consider how the 'world' of young people may be influencing the ideas and beliefs of those you are or will be having conversations about sex with. They will also help you consider the impact of these on your expectations of conversations and your own approach to the topic. The 'inside out' questions encourage you to think about what you're bringing to the conversation that can increase a young person's awareness, engage their curiosity, build their confidence, develop their skills and grow their character in relation to this particular area. These discussion pointers can be used for your own reflective practice or in supporting discussion among youth work volunteers and the parents/carers of the young people you serve.

Part 2

Part 2 introduces a framework that not only underpins how we have conversations but also takes seriously the young people's God-created journey into sexual maturity. It both focuses on how young people explore and experience aspects of sex and gives you some wisdom around how to ask questions that open up conversations around these key issues. Each young person's way into conversations about sex is unique, shaped by his or her own experiences, family environment, wider cultural or faith values and broader societal ideals. Each conversation with a young person about sex is unique too. We have the glorious task of releasing emerging generations into the possibility of living sexually whole lives with God at the centre.

Part 3

Part 3 contains the complete findings from online surveys and conversations with Christian young people and youth leaders in the UK. A total of 551 young people in the UK aged between 16 and 21 who self-identified as Christian, took part in A Christian Youth Sex Survey, and 318 Christian youth leaders in the UK took part in The Big Sex Chat online survey. I'm deeply grateful to everyone who took the time to share their experiences, insights and perspectives with me. These have been rich listening exercises. Sometimes, the findings confirmed what I suspected; sometimes they surprised me. Either way, it's worth noting that although they aren't representative of *all* Christian young people in the UK, they provide a timely window into the shifting ideas, beliefs and needs of young people in our church communities or families. As always, we need to keep listening to young people, to keep asking the right questions not just about what they face but also about how we listen to them.

Throughout the book, I refer to some of the findings of these surveys, but in Part 3 you can see the results for yourself and draw your own conclusions from this sample of young people and youth leaders.

Exposed

This book comes to you with a fair amount of trepidation. It took a chat with a trusted friend, who reminded me that fear of saying the wrong thing is a cultural narrative that should never silence us, to get me to commit pen to paper. As a white, straight, cisgender, married woman raised in the West, I recognize that there are times when I write about things I have not experienced or wrestled with from the inside. Personal experiences play a powerful role in shaping our theology and youth ministry practice, so I seek to draw on a range of diverse voices of both leaders and young people in this book. I am grateful to them for being willing to be part of this conversation.

I write things that you may resonate with, things you can agree with and wholeheartedly stand behind. It's equally possible that I'm going to say things that might question what you think, or what you think of me and where I sit on these strange lines of conservative, progressive, pro, against. I'm probably going to fight those labels quite hard. I don't think they're particularly helpful because they tend to emphasize our differences rather than our common need for the grace and salvation Jesus alone offers.

When it comes to our conversations with young people about sex, the gospel isn't that God can stop young people thinking about sex or having sex, but that God can make young people holy. Our job isn't to produce polite, well-behaved, religious people. It's to grow followers of Jesus who become part of the transforming work of God in the world. This is our hope and our motivation to wade into areas we might feel uncertain or even uncomfortable in.

In this book and in all our conversations about sex, I'm eager that we as leaders wear God's name well. That we're honest with our wrestling and reading of Scripture, open to challenge and correction, willing to change our minds and to never speak about what we're not prepared to do. Whatever side of debate around biblical sexual ethics we might find ourselves on, let's see ourselves on the same side – the side of loving precious, unique, diverse and phenomenal young people and walking them towards holiness. Let's be *for* young people; for their healthy sexual development, safe relationships, faithfulness to each other; for them exploring and integrating godly practices into their lives. Let's be *for* costly discipleship that runs hard after Jesus, and knows the stubborn grace of God, where no topic is out of bounds and no young person is asked to leave. And let's be *for* each other when we agree or disagree in our humble handling of Scripture, trusting the Bible to challenge us and the Spirit to convict us.

Talking together

There will be times, as there always have been in Church history, when the unity of the Church is hotly contested. When it feels better to split than to hold together. Jesus never asked us to get along nicely; he asks us to *love* each other, and in loving each other to demonstrate to the world that Christ is the Messiah (John 17.20–23). For the sake of the emerging generations, let's hold space for each other as we seek God's grace for our own lives and the lives of the young people we're called to serve.

Over the years, I've become increasingly aware of the cognitive dissonance happening for many Christian teens between the sex education they receive in school or online (which is unaffected by the gospel) and their loving and non-judging posture toward sexual minorities (which has the gospel all over it). Much of their hunger for holiness is untouched by a Church that is obsessed with calling out the 'wrong' views on sex, yet many of their questions are left unanswered. Instead of accusing one another, we need to hold space for each other's differing views and concentrate on being the safe, Spirit-filled servants that young people need us to be. The question I'd love you to carry in your heart as you read this book is, 'How can I have conversations about sex with these young people that help them grow in their love for Jesus and to be more open to the work of the Spirit in transforming their lives?'

As I finished the 'phone sex thing' conversation, I thought how extraordinary it was that a young person would seek me out to process this experience. I felt deeply humbled, and slightly in awe of her and others of her generation who dare to believe that God is big enough for all the conversations that need to take place.

I asked the young people I surveyed whether they thought the Church should be teaching Christian young people about sex. Ninety-four per cent said yes. Then I asked them what they'd like the Church to make space to talk with them about. The top three responses were: 1) how to have healthy relationships; 2) what the Bible teaches about sex; 3) setting sexual boundaries in premarital relationships. These young people aren't mirroring youth culture. From mass media and the entertainment industry to the porn industry, nothing in wider culture is supporting young people to know how to be a Christian in today's world. So when asked what they want the Church to teach them about sex, they did three remarkable things: 1) they immediately placed sex in the context of relationships more generally; 2) they instinctively pivoted towards God's word to be a guide; 3) they placed sex primarily in the context of marriage. I mean, what does *that* tell us?

In many ways, it's hard to know. Young Christians who take the time to fill in a survey that they know is geared towards a Christian approach to sex may be more inclined to answer in a certain way. More females than males filled it in. These and other factors need to be considered before we make blanket statements based on the results of a survey. But let me tell you what I think it points to: we have an emerging generation of young people exploring Christian faith who get that following Jesus will mark them out as radically different in how they demonstrate love for others and a life of holiness. I write this book for these extraordinary young people who are daily having to choose Jesus in ways I never did as a teenager, as well as all those who right now don't know that God is with and for them. If conversations with you or me about phone sex, or porn, or being gay, or masturbation, or coercion, or kissing, or falling in love, or being broken-hearted, or fancying someone to distraction or sex with robots can take young people a little further along the road to discovering the life God planned for them to know, why would we not be prepared to go there?

So let's go there – with kindness, boldness and restraint. With kindness because anything done without love isn't of God. With boldness because who we are in Christ invites us into a life that we need courage to face, and with restraint because, without it, we can hurt each other. I'm glad to be opening up this important conversation with you.

Yours with kindness, boldness and restraint,

Rachel x

Part 1

The teaching I received in church gave me a clear understanding of
no sex before marriage. I lived it religiously, not gracefully. I wasn't
kind to others who weren't able to hold this, and I was jealous of
those who didn't have this restriction.
Matt, UK youth leader

Purity was really important in my youth group and was idolized
particularly in women and girls. It was definitely linked to self-
worth and a sense of wholeness. I felt I had more chance of meeting
'The One' if I abstained from sexual temptation.
Hana, UK youth leader

You yourselves used to be in the darkness, but since you have
become the Lord's people, you are in the light. So you must live like
people who belong to the light, for it is the light that brings a rich
harvest of every kind of goodness, righteousness, and truth.
Ephesians 5.8–10 (MSG)

1

The purity hangover

If you've ever had a hangover, you'll know what I'm talking about. The nausea. The headache. The lethargy and dry mouth. You ask yourself questions like, 'Why did I drink so much?' You come to conclusions like, 'That last glass or three just wasn't worth it.' You find yourself making resolutions like, 'I'm not drinking alcohol ever again.' When we're experiencing the effects of a hangover, we need a period of recovery. We'll all bring different remedies to the table (raw egg, pills, copious amounts of water, the complete *Friends* box set), but what unites us is a desire to put ourselves back together and to feel all right again.

As well as individuals experiencing hangovers from a heavy night of drinking, churches can feel hangovers from heavy cultural movements that don't do us or the gospel much good. We're in one such moment – and understanding this moment (what brought us here and why) will help us reimagine conversations with young people about sex.

Our recovery is from the purity culture that sprung up in the USA in the 1990s and took root in the Protestant Evangelical community in the UK. At its heart is a desire to promote sexual abstinence outside marriage, a view shared by most Christian traditions around the world. But some groups began pushing an agenda on young people that the Bible requires strict roles for males and females, including no masturbation, no dating, no holding hands and absolutely no kissing before marriage.

Much has been written over the past few years about the damage this has caused in young people's lives. One of the most powerful critiques found how the purity culture in the USA negatively affects girls the most:

While boys are taught that their minds are a gateway to sin, women are taught that their bodies are. After years of being told that they're responsible for not only their own purity, but the purity of the men

17

and boys around them; and of associating sexual desire with depravity and shame, those feelings often haunt women's relationships with their bodies for a lifetime.[1]

Many churches with youth groups across the UK bought into the purity movement or used it to reinforce a 'don't do it!' approach to teaching young people about sex. It was a legalism born of a theology that somewhere along the line capitulated to the idea of salvation by works – you need to earn your salvation by being good.

Now in his thirties, Sam reflects on being a teenage boy in a church that took a very hard line on sex before marriage:

> The legalistic theology my peers at church and I grew up with made the struggles of adolescence we were going through so much worse. No sex before marriage meant no kissing, no dating, no holding hands and absolutely no wanking. The leaders taught this as divine revelation. I was a young lad who was growing up wanting to please God *and* those leaders, so what they said was a big deal. As teaching goes, that's guaranteed failure that leads to deep shame. I began to believe that bad stuff was happening to me because I couldn't stop wanking. I even remember thinking, 'If only I can stop wanking, the bullying at school will stop.' I had no healthy sense of what was happening to me, so I learned that the only way to survive in church was to lie when I was asked the difficult questions.

Dangerous double standards

Where the teaching was twinned with a repressed view of women's sexuality, it often led to young people internalizing damaging double standards around sex; girls weren't seen as sexual so were never talked to about masturbation, porn or sexual desire. Instead, they were told to avoid all behaviour that would inspire a boy to think about sex or want to have sex with them: 'You're responsible for yourself and the boys. Your sexuality is unlocked at marriage.' Boys, on the other hand, were seen as overly sexual, and told they are more prone to sexual thoughts and feelings: 'When you think about having sex with a girl, don't masturbate because then you're defiling her when you should be viewing her as your sister. God's best for you is to find a girl who has saved her virginity for you. Girls who have had sex before marriage are both sexually and emotionally broken.'

Alongside these explicit (or implied) ideas, there were other topics young people growing up in church weren't hearing, and still don't hear, talked about. As well as the classic avoidance of talking about porn or masturbation, Wongani (a youth worker now in his twenties) observes that, growing up in church, he never heard teaching on sexual safety, abuse, controlling behaviours or exploitation:

I was led to believe that if a man acted out in an 'impure' manner towards a woman who was dressed 'inappropriately', then this was partially her fault, as the man can't resist seeing her in a sexualized manner. I rarely heard teaching from a female perspective, which meant I assumed that female desire for sex was less that the male desire.

This isn't new. For generations, the Church has had a messed-up relationship with female sexuality. Tertullian, one of the early church fathers, said of women: 'You are the devil's gateway . . . You destroyed so easily God's image, man. On account of your desert – that is, death – even the son of God had to die.'[2] Many of the early church fathers saw women (who were associated with all things carnal) as evil because they trapped men (who were associated with all things spiritual) in sinful flesh (having sex).

Interestingly, in my conversations with youth leaders in the UK, it wasn't just women but also men who spoke of internalizing a deep shame as adolescents about their bodies and sexuality. When young Christians receive purity teaching with little or no understanding of why or how to achieve this, they are more likely to consider that all their sexual thoughts and feelings are impure and sinful. The negative impact of this reductive teaching around sex is one from which many Christian youth workers and pastors I meet (myself included) are still healing. But this approach is especially harmful for young people going through sexual development and the shaping of their identity.

Although the starting point for these approaches may have ideas found in Scripture, the application of these behavioural codes and the way adherence is expected and normalized in church communities increases the possibility of young people being hurt rather than helped. By positioning extreme abstinence as 'choosing God' and questioning or rejecting part or all of it as 'rejecting God', young people feel they are faced with a stark choice: stick unquestioningly to the rules about sex and you're loved by the Church and by God; push back against or transgress these rules and you won't be. It's no wonder some young people find it psychologically less painful to walk away from the Church than to stay connected to a community where they feel unable to live up to this standard of 'being a Christian'.

This is borne out in The Big Sex Chat. The data suggests that 22 per cent of youth leaders who responded think their church's approach to teaching young people about sex has a positive impact, 57 per cent a negative impact and 21 per cent it's either mixed, neutral or unknown. In comparing the categories of positive and negative, some interesting patterns emerge. For example, half of the responses describing a negative impact relate to shame, and nearly half of all of the comments with a positive tone (42 per cent) talk about how their church creates safe, shame-free spaces where young people can have honest conversations. In unpacking what the youth leaders who responded meant by a 'negative' impact, the comments seemed to fall into one of four distinct categories: 17 per cent said they felt the teaching of their church around sex damaged young people, 22 per cent said the silence in itself presented sex as negative, 23 per cent said they felt it drove young people away from the Church and from God, and 30 per cent said it loaded shame on young people.

It's possible to roughly summarize the youth leaders' responses to the impact of their church's teaching about sex into the following statements:

- Our church teaches a conservative biblical view and we think it is helpful for young people.
- Our church prioritizes open and reflective conversation and we think it is helpful for young people.

- Our church teaches a conservative biblical view and we think it is damaging for young people.
- Our church is mostly silent on the topic and we think it is damaging for young people.
- Our church doesn't have a position or we don't know what it is.[3]

As this data shows, it's not just the 'extreme abstinence' approach that causes damage. Many churches who wouldn't go as far as saying that dating or kissing before marriage is a sin have been heavily influenced by poor theology that puts too much emphasis on teenage virginity. I remember being shown a picture of male and female stick figures with boxes covering their torsos and the slogan, 'Don't touch what's in the box!' The message was that your main job as a Christian young person was to be vigilant about your virginity, avoiding anything (I was never clear what behaviours this included) that would defile the perfection Jesus wanted you to achieve. Tragically and inevitably, this just encouraged young Christians to go underground with their questions, guilt and confusion. In her book, *Real Sex*, Lauren Winner challenges the idea that orientating a Christian sexual ethic around virginity 'is to turn sexual purity and sexual sin into a light switch you can flip. One day you're sexually righteous, and the next day after illicit loss of your virginity, you're a sinner.'[4]

A fixation on virginity as a benchmark for sexual purity means that, rather than arming Christian young people with a biblical vision for their sexuality that equips and empowers them to live sexually whole lives, they're kept in a state of enforced sexual ignorance. Ignorance is not innocence. And even if it was, innocence is not the goal for teaching Christian young people a biblical sexual ethic.

This don't-do-it-and-certainly-don't-talk-about-it approach to sexuality has cast a long shadow over many of our adult lives and relationships. If one of the main goals of teaching a biblical sexual ethic is to protect young people from the physical, emotional and spiritual harm of sexual activity outside marriage, it doesn't work. In many cases it makes young people more vulnerable to poor sexual choices and the harm of deep shame about their sexual selves, leaving them in need of sexual health services but less likely to access them. It also means that young people are ill-equipped to negotiate their own growing sexual awareness when they're with their peers who are beginning to engage in sexual activity.

In my conversations with youth workers, many talked about how painfully naïve about sex they were when they went to college or university. For some it meant that they found themselves in sexually compromised situations where they struggled to assert choice or even appreciate what was happening to them. When the main message is to avoid all sexual activity with little or no guidance as to how or why, it can lead to young people in our churches to feel disconnected from their bodies.

James talked about how this disconnect with his body meant that: 'the first time I was having sex I didn't realize I was having sex. Things had gradually started to happen and then you realize, oh, this is happening. I was so disconnected that I was almost embarrassed that this is what my body did.'

And it's not only adult Christians who speak of experiencing a damaging script about their bodies and capacity for sexual feeling. When asked to describe the main message they hear from church about sex, the majority of respondents in the youth survey (65 per cent) said, 'God is disappointed if Christians have sex outside marriage.' Although more Christian young people (48 per cent) were *for* the church teaching young people about not having sex outside of marriage (31 per cent were against), they were clear that the church could do this a whole lot better.

> I think we should be taught biblically how God views sex and what and why it was created; however, I don't believe the church should teach young people that if they have had sex they're a 'bad' person.

> It would be more helpful if churches talked about the heart of Jesus, and in knowing him you will be far more likely to understand what he's saying.

> Don't teach sex in a hard and fast way that leads to condemnation.

These comments were from Christian young people who believe that it's *right* that the church should teach them not to have sex outside marriage. They aren't against the historic Christian view. What they're against is the shaming and condemnation that comes with it. This sort of hardline teaching also fails in that it doesn't actually change attitudes to sex outside marriage. A piece of research by the Pew Research Centre in 2020 found that roughly one third of US Christians think it's acceptable to have sex outside marriage. That's a huge figure for the nation that brought the purity industry to the world, and highlights that external rules rarely change internal attitudes.[5] The Apostle Paul wouldn't have been surprised by this. In his letter to the new church in Colossae, he reminds them of the pointlessness of a rule-based ethic that doesn't have any impact on the desires of someone's heart and will (Colossians 2.20–23).

Legalism always raises Pharisees, not disciples. When the church teaches about sex in a way that doesn't invite or allow for compassionate conversations, we're in danger of hurting each other and creating the context for ongoing hurt and judgement. A church-based youth leader in the UK put it like this:

> The young people in the church see it as a rule they have to follow because they've been told to – there's no actual independent, personal commitment being made. They automatically go to 'How far is too far?' and they quickly gossip if they find out that someone in the youth group has 'done stuff'. Then they see them as a bad person and the hypocrisy increases.

So where does this leave us now? What is the legacy of purity culture in how churches in the UK engage with young people in conversations about sex?

Unintended consequences

For all the helpful critique of sexual purity teaching, there are some important questions we still need to ask about what the entrenched certainty of the past is being replaced by. In rejecting a movement that sought hard and fast maps for young people to plot their path towards sexual purity, how are we seeking to wisely navigate a third way between a legalism that crushes and condemns and a liberalism that denies the unique radical distinctiveness of the gospel?

I put this to Christian youth leaders working in the UK church or in parachurch youth organizations in the online survey. Of the 318 who responded, 53 per cent felt that churches are increasingly realizing the need for more open conversations and pastoral support of young people in their youth ministries. But 28 per cent felt that this was impaired by the reality that many churches are more likely to pull back from these conversations for fear of causing hurt.

> Oftentimes churches can't decide what they believe so don't know how to engage with young people on this topic. They would rather it was forgotten or left up to the parents to deal with.

The youth leader of another church spoke of the church being 'too scared of uproar'.

This fear of getting it wrong was a common theme. 'We are hesitant because the culture is changing so rapidly and we're not sure how to keep up.' This inevitably leads to a cycle of not talking with young people in church about sex (see Figure 1).

Breaking The Cycle (of not talking about sex...)

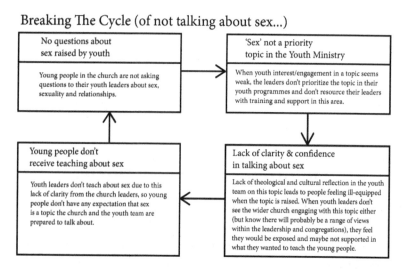

Figure 1 **Breaking the cycle (of not talking about sex . . .)**

Unsurprisingly, where churches *are* engaging young people in conversations about sex, it seems to be reactive rather than proactive. Of those who responded, the most frequently reported contexts for conversations are when a young person raises it in a one-to-one session (46 per cent) and when a related situation arises in the youth group (45 per cent). Only 13 per cent said that the topic of sex *never* comes up in their work with young people. It would seem, therefore, that where good relationships are built between young people and safe adults in church, some young people feel confident to raise the subject.

Although this is good news, we need to consider whether *more* young people in these settings would appreciate greater intentionality around having these conversations. Only 4 per cent of youth leaders say they frequently initiate conversations with young people on these issues, and when asked why this is the case, the most frequently stated reason is that the young people aren't asking questions, so the leaders feel it inappropriate to raise it (38 per cent).

But how do we *know* what young people might want to ask unless we create the safe space for these questions to surface? In seeking to protect young people from hard and fast rules that set them up to fail, we're seemingly relying on young people's courage to risk raising the questions *without knowing what might happen when they do.*

There's something really interesting going on here. It seems that youth and church leaders do want to have kind, godly, open conversations with young people about sex, but perhaps don't often initiate the space or opportunities for them to happen. Because of this, when conversations do surface, they happen at times when there may well be safeguarding issues involved, possibly adding to the fear that conversations about sex will expose the youth leader and their youth group to significant challenges. This means that any engagement that happens with the wider youth group about sex is overshadowed by the specifics of one young person, making open debate and discussion inappropriate, unsafe and ineffective. Added to this, if you're a youth leader who is 'aware that within the congregation, adults hold really different views on this topic', you will feel a certain hesitation to speak for fear of the wider church's response.

But even with all these challenges, there are many youth leaders and churches that are creating space for conversations with young people about sex. When asked what motivates them, 79 per cent said it was their desire for young people not to feel shame and confusion, and to know a safe space to ask their questions. Unsurprisingly, then, in a list of topics considered by youth leaders as important to cover, physical and emotional safety came top of the list, followed closely by consent, handling guilt and shame and issues of intimacy. What came bottom of the list was sexual integrity and sexual purity. This raises interesting questions as to why this is the case and what it might take for us to rehabilitate our thinking around holiness and to restore our confidence in the radical invitation of the gospel when it comes to our sex lives.

In many ways, we're at ground zero. What we do now could be hugely significant for how future generations connect their faith with sex. In his excellent book, *Faith Generation*, Nick Shepherd argues that young people need not only to make sense of their own faith, but also to see how being a person of faith helps them to make sense of the world around them.[6] Post purity movement, how might we reimagine with young people a biblical sexual ethic that takes their journey seriously and offers them deep encounters with the transforming power of God as well as opportunities to explore their questions within a loving Christian community?

Signposts, not maps

For starters, let's avoid hard and fast maps for young people. These invariably lead to simplistic equations, and simplistic equations don't ring true when it comes to sex and relationships. We all know that God doesn't 'owe' us the partner of our dreams if we promise not to have sex outside marriage. Many devoted disciples don't ever marry. Dating a non-Christian doesn't automatically mean you will lose your faith (nor that they will become a Christian). Being straight doesn't mean all your sexual desires honour God. This is not to suggest that these aren't important areas of youth ministry. It's because they are important that we must avoid at all costs making out that human sexuality is straightforward. Human sexuality is incredibly complicated and often difficult to navigate. As those who embrace a relentlessly positive view of sex as God designed it, we need to offer young people something more meaningful than trite answers that don't compute with life.

But rejecting easy answers doesn't mean that we should be silent. A silent church is a neglectful church. We minister to young people in the reality that: 'there are certain ways of behaving that are so out of line with how God made the world, and humans in particular, that they bring their own nemesis. Sexual behaviour certainly comes into that category.'[7] It's important that the church is armed with knowledge and compassion to support young people to order their sex lives in ways that see them flourishing as divine image bearers.

Jesus places a high call on the lives of his followers. It's a call to obedience to the Father. This is the relationship that enables us to rightly order our sexual lives. Peter put it this way: 'As obedient children, let yourselves be pulled into a way of life shaped by God's life, a life energetic and blazing with holiness' (1 Peter 1.15). Failure to engage with young people on what this means in their lives would be to abandon them to a culture that doesn't acknowledge or hallow their God-given worth and potential as sexual beings made in God's image.

Paul, in his letter to the church in Corinth, encourages young disciples to jump on the ride of their lives, to get curious and eager for what God is doing in their lives, 'perfecting holiness out of reverence for God' (2 Corinthians 7.1, NIV). We are absolutely accepted *by* God and we yield an absolute surrender *to* God. *This* is the paradigm that can frame every conversation we ever have with young people about sex. *This* is the holiness narrative that enables us to reimagine conversations that have at their heart a desire for each young person to grow in love for Jesus and in sexual well-being.

Outside in; inside out

Outside in

- How have you been influenced by the teaching about sex you received as a teenager?
- What's your reflection on the critique of the purity movement in this chapter?
- What cultural narratives about young people and sex are you most affected by?

- When have you blocked or prevented conversations with young people about sex, and what caused this?
- How has the wider culture of the Church contributed to this?
- What have you seen or what do you know to be the impact of this on young people?
- Where and when have you felt closed down by others, and what impact has this had on you?
- What topics to do with sex are most likely to have been closed down or blocked in your family or church?
- Why has this been the case? Can you name the fears that lie behind this blocking of certain topics?
- What form did that blocking or closing down of conversation take?

Inside out

- When have you had your best conversations with young people about sex?
- What did you need to do to ensure these could happen?
- How have you helped young people feel safe to ask questions about sex?
- How might creating more opportunities for young people to encounter God's presence as they face these questions enable them to connect their faith with their sexuality?
- How have you experienced God's goodness and guidance in your own life in relation to sex and relationships?
- What have you needed to accept about your own story of sexuality, sex and relationships?
- What might you still need to accept?
- What might you need to let go of?
- If you resonate with the idea of needing a deeper healing from damaging or misguided teaching on sex, how might you want to move forward with this?
- Who could support you?

2

Rising strong

A few years ago, I thought I had killed my youth group.

Not literally. But I'd just taken over the teen girls' group at church and made that fatal error of changing the night of the weekly meeting. True to form, everyone came on the wrong night, and (yes, it gets worse) I failed to show up on said night to remind them about the change of day, so no one came on the actual night. Realizing my mistake, I sent numerous messages via home visits, WhatsApp, Facebook, text, postcards and sky writing. But the silence was deafening.

The following week, the team and I stood in the cold church doorway, watching, waiting and imagining that it was all over. But it wasn't!

Suddenly, young people stumbled out of the foggy darkness into the slightly less cold church hall, where we ate too many doughnuts and talked about porn. It got me to thinking that there are so many other things young people could be doing than rocking up to one of the youth things youth leaders put on. Our sofas might be harbouring a million strands of bacteria, the snooker table is pretty ropey, and no one has seen the Xbox or dance mat for years (thank goodness), but still they come. OK, maybe in smaller numbers than we'd like, but they show up. Why?

Maybe it's because we take the time to really 'see' and then reflect back to them an image of themselves that they don't glimpse in many other places. Maybe it's because we emphasize real connection and communication. Zara summed it up: 'I feel close to my friends when we're messaging each other, but here in the group it's even more close.' Maybe it's because we're not afraid of the teenage years. Instead of dreading them, we are the people who love to make space for the most precious, precarious, powerful years of adolescence.

Young people have some very important work to do during adolescence: the hard graft of working out who they are. Erik Erikson, the renowned psychologist, writing in the 1960s, described eight stages of life, from birth to death, each with its own major conflict to resolve. The fifth stage, occurring in adolescence (between the ages of approximately twelve and eighteen), which Erikson called 'identity versus role confusion', is about the formation of a strong, independent sense of self.[1] The question, put simply, is nothing less than, *who am I?*

Who am I?

This 'who am I?' question breaks down into a series of important areas: What am I good at? What do I like? What do I believe? Who do I believe in? What do other people think of me? What am I capable of achieving? Where do I come from?

Erikson believed that young people who receive proper encouragement from those around them to engage in this self-exploration will emerge from this stage with a strong sense of self and a feeling of independence and control. Those who miss out on this kind of support are more likely to remain confused about themselves into their future. We aren't required to become psychologists to observe that, as young people make the vital transition from childhood to adulthood, many begin to feel an increased confusion or insecurity about themselves and how they are perceived by others. Their behaviour may seem suddenly quite unpredictable and impulsive: one summer they're a full-on Disney princess but by September they're a goth. One minute they're praying with their friends after the service and the next they're posting on social media about being an atheist. Experimenting with different roles and behaviours is all part of the process of finding a sense of personal identity. Finding ways to exclude and reject parents and other authority figures is also a necessary part of severing ties and establishing their own identity. Although the family may continue to exert an influence on how young people in this life stage feel about themselves, friends, social groups, peers, societal trends and popular culture take more of a lead in shaping and forming a young person's sense of who they are.

The identity chair

I once heard the process of adolescent identity formation being described along the lines of building a chair. The four legs represent the four key developmental areas of conflict that must be resolved in childhood around our ability to trust, our sense of autonomy, our ability to instigate activity among peers and our recognition that there are things we can do. The conflict unique to adolescence rests precariously on these four psychological building blocks, like the seat of a chair rest on the four chair legs. The existential question of 'who am I?' balances on all that has been internalized so far about how safe the world is along with their own sense of adequacy, competence and purpose. In today's climate of unparalleled pressure to conform to very prescribed ideals of perfectionism, this exploration of who they are can lead to an emotionally and mentally painful experience as young people fear that, whoever they are, they're never ever going to be 'enough'. Not good enough, not clever enough, not pretty enough, not athletic enough, not 'Christian' enough, not popular enough. Because of this, it's crucial that we appreciate what's happening for young people and, even with the questions and concerns it may raise for us, that we take their identity formation seriously.

So how do young people today form their sense of self? What steers do they find in wider culture and their peer groups?

Consumer culture bombards young people with the idea that, because their desires are the best guide to who they are, they alone know their true identity. At the same time, it paints the perfect life that everyone else seems to be excelling at – everyone except, of course, the one young person scrolling through all these tweaked, staged, faked or filtered images. A common theme on social media is not comparing yourself to others, which is ironic seeing as the platform is the best vehicle for stirring up mass malcontent. The way to reach this goal of self-fulfilment is to 'figure out who you really are, because once you do, you'll be less likely to feel shaken up by what other people are doing'.[2]

There is wisdom in this. Comparison is a killer, for all of us. Our uniqueness is something to embrace, not to be apologetic for. But what does it mean for young people to work out who they 'really are'? Who gets to help them in this? One fourteen-year-old sagely told me recently, 'No one gets to say who you should be. What matters most is your own opinion of yourself, and the affirmation you give yourself. No one else matters in this equation.'

Sadly, this quasi-truth weaponizes a young person's identity exploration against them. By presenting the idea that you only know yourself in isolation from others and that your desires are your best guide to figuring out who you are, young people are robbed of the truth that we discover who we are in relationship with others. It's as we grow, take risks, form friendships, make choices, face consequences, receive feedback, become aware of our deeper desires and develop habits that we discover that who we are isn't determined by what we feel on any one day, but rather by what we believe about our purpose and how we define our goals, values and ideals. All that takes time to develop and requires a strong network of relationships to help draw these to our attention and to encourage us as we invest in what matters to us. In a sense, we can say that identity is both achieved (this is who I am becoming through my choices, decisions, beliefs, etc.) and received (this is how other people experience me and reflect to me aspects of who I am). This doesn't happen overnight.

Emerging faith identity

For young people growing up in the church, one of the questions they have to resolve is how far Christian faith will shape their emerging identity. The radical invitation at the heart of the gospel is to come to Jesus to be defined, not to come to Jesus to have your definition of yourself affirmed. It's a call to come to Jesus and die to yourself. But this presents conflict both with the culture at large that prioritizes self-identification free from external influences and with the culture in church that prioritizes adherence to a set of doctrinal beliefs or statements. Young people's tendency to challenge the status quo can provoke anxiety in a church that sees issues of faith identity in certain ways.

I regularly hear parents and youth leaders say with huge exasperation, 'I just want them to know who they are in Christ. They're all over the place right now!' We want young people to face the challenges of adolescent identity formation from the security of belonging to God. But finding their identity in Christ doesn't remove them from the stage of adolescent identity formation. And pushing back against the faith they've inherited is part of the process. Although there may be safeguarding concerns to be responsive to, young people being 'all over the place' isn't in itself the problem. In fact, it might be the very place where young people find themselves in God's appreciation of them and purpose for them. The problem comes when they're abandoned to do this alone, or they internalize the idea that doubt, changing their minds, gathering information and examining the evidence is *contrary* to a faith identity formation.

Sometimes, I've been guilty of encouraging young people to examine the Christian faith they've grown up with *in order to get to the point where they can then commit to being a Christian*. As if having questions is what happens *before* you commit to Jesus. But Erikson would put it very differently: if we want to encourage maturity in faith, we need to encourage the testing and examination of everything.[3] These are not the practices of those on the outside looking in; rather, this is what people who are on a journey of deepening faith identity do. In his four stages of faith formation, John Westerhoff talks about the 'Searching Faith' stage (common in late adolescence), which comprises doubt and deep questioning of the faith you're being raised in, as well as experimentation with alternative understandings and ways as you begin to choose for yourself whether you will commit to this identity or not.[4] In her research into the relationship between adolescent identity formation and faith maturity, Jayce Long concluded, 'A valid measure of faith maturity should include exploration, commitment, and integration, but the exploration has to be balanced within the commitment, or the commitment will not produce behaviour associated with that commitment.'[5] If this is true, then the meaning we attribute to what we see really matters.

Let's say a super-devout twelve-year-old in the church youth group rocks up one week sounding like the biggest atheist on the planet. Is he a backslider? Or a seventeen-year-old who last year had a life-changing experience at youth camp now struggles to read the Bible because she read something online about it being against gay people and she's angry. Is she on the edge of faith? The first may go on to be an atheist for the rest of his life. The second may walk away from one congregation and find another in which to continue her journey of faith. We're not to know that. But it's also true that they're both at significant moments in their Christian faith formation where their doubts, examinations and questions need to be embraced by the wider community of faith as signs of growth, not signs of wilful disobedience and rejection of God. If we can see this stage as offering a unique time for us to help young people find ways to connect their real experiences with who God is and who God says they are, we are more likely to want to find ways to appropriately and compassionately agitate and excavate questions in safe, positive and helpful ways. We'll also do better at provoking all young people in our churches to search deeply the stuff that really matters. 'You'll find me,' God promises. 'As you look for me with all your heart, you'll find me and be found in me' (see Jeremiah 29.13).

Sexual identity

In my experience, lots of those 'who am I?' questions for young people in a Christian community often hinge on issues of sexual identity. This is not surprising, because we live in a culture in the West where sexual practice is understood to be the outward expression of an essential inner nature, meaning that sexual feelings often take prominence when it comes to an individual's self-identification.

Interestingly, the idea that our sexual desires are fixed and exclusive is being challenged among emerging generations who are embracing a sexual fluidity that is more about a movement to be part of than simply a label for sexual attraction. Since the turn of the millennium, the term 'queer' has been increasingly embraced as an 'umbrella term for people who ascribe to non-normative sexual and gender identities'.[6] Popular TV presenter, columnist and NHS doctor Dr Ranj Singh explains, 'Queer, to me, now means the freedom to express yourself and to express your love in a way that you choose.'[7]

'I would describe myself as a bisexual homoromantic,' Alice, aged twenty-three, told *The Guardian*:

> 'It means I like sex with men and women, but I only fall in love with women. I wouldn't say something wishy-washy like, "It's all about the person," because more often it's just that I sometimes like a penis.' She says her attitude towards sex and sexuality is similar among other people in her peer group. 'A lot of my friends talk about their sexuality in terms of behaviour these days, rather than in terms of

labels. So they'll say, "I like boys", or "I get with girls too," rather than saying, "I'm gay, I'm a lesbian, I'm bisexual."[8]

As well as negotiating a rapidly changing cultural narrative about sexual identity, young people are experiencing a growing awareness of their own sexual response and desires. Some young people experience exclusive sexual attraction (to the same sex or to the opposite sex); some young people experience non-exclusive sexual attraction, meaning their sexual attractions might change. It's possible that sexual attractions can change during adolescence and even throughout their lifetime.

In a lecture, Professor of Psychology and Gender Studies, Dr Lisa Diamond, shares how sexual attractions aren't as exclusive as people have come to believe.[9] In her research, around 14 per cent of women and 7 per cent of men reported experiencing same-sex attraction, but less than 2 per cent of women and less than 1 per cent of men were exclusively same-sex attracted throughout their lives. Fifty per cent of self-identified heterosexual women and 25 per cent of heterosexual men reported having experienced a same-sex attraction in the past year, and 35 per cent of women and 24 per cent of men reported a same-sex sexual fantasy. Although sexual attractions can be flexible on their own, there's no evidence that forcing a change in sexual attraction works. In fact, it is psychologically damaging, and many Christians who used to teach so-called conversion therapy practices have stopped, and some even campaign against it. It would also be wrong to use this to draw the conclusion that a young person experiencing same-sex attraction is just going through 'a phase'.

But what about the idea of sexual sin? Are sexual desires for someone of the opposite sex always honouring to God? Is it sinful to be attracted to someone of the same sex? The Bible makes no such claim. Irrespective of the direction of our sexual attraction, we're all invited into the community of believers who are saved by faith in Jesus alone. Because of this, we all need the work of the Spirit to sanctify us and to help us live lives that glorify God.

Our sexual desires in and of themselves are not sinful. But there's a difference between experiencing sexual desires and how we seek to express or fulfil those desires. The Bible is clear that lust is sinful, because lusting is a choice to pursue someone sexually in our minds whom we are not free to desire. 'But I say: Anyone who even looks at a woman with lust in his eye has already committed adultery with her in his heart' (Matthew 5.28, TLB).

The challenge for us to work through with Christian young people (irrespective of sexual identity labels) is how they examine and express their desires in line with their beliefs and identity as followers of Jesus. This is a deeply sensitive area that we need to venture into with profound concern for each young person's welfare. It is highly likely that young people in church who experience same-sex or both-sex attraction will have carried this growing knowledge for a long time and will be vulnerable to feeling shame and rejection by both the Christian community they've grown up in and the God they love, who may be the only source of comfort they have right now.

> By far the most helpful thing for me as a gay teenager in church was having a youth worker who was so humble and invested in the bigger picture with me. Before all else, he wanted to help me love Jesus more. I would come with all these questions and carrying all my fear of what I was sharing with him. He always met me with kindness and patience. He was conservative in his understanding of sex (I was less so at the time) but he resisted the anxiety to quickly assert what the Bible said or the church thought. I think that would have been too much too soon for me. I needed someone to do the groundwork with me of helping me understand that I was fully loved by God. I needed that before I was ready to grapple with any of the big issues of discipleship – all of them, not just about my sexuality. I remember one time I was pouring out my misery and confusion and he said, 'I wish I had the magic words that could make this all feel OK for you. I wish I knew all the answers. I don't. But I'm in this for the long haul with you and I'll try to find the answers with you.' Such humility gives tremendous room for God's Spirit to work at the right pace and towards the right goal. He was so often a manifestation of God's grace in my life and his humility and gentleness helped keep me in church when I could have so easily slipped away. He perfected the ministry of holding his tongue![10]

Some of the most powerful changes in my life have resulted from conversations with others who love me and love Jesus. But more often than not, the most significant moments of transformation have been instigated by the Holy Spirit and in his timing – and often without other people getting in involved. When we jump to filling in the gaps for young people with what we think and what we believe, we sometimes drown out the very voice they need to hear most. Helping a young person foster a desire to listen to Jesus enables them to discover a more meaningful faith and opens them up to the deep work that only Jesus can do.

If we cannot provide young people in our churches with opportunities for safe, compassionate and ongoing conversations (where we do a whole lot of listening) around this issue, then we cannot be presenting our view of biblical teaching on same-sex, sexually intimate relationships. Jesus is pretty stark on this: 'And you experts in the law, woe to you, because you load people down with burdens they can hardly carry, and you yourselves will not lift one finger to help them' (Luke 11.46, NIV). Whatever our convictions of a biblical sexual ethic, we must never lose sight (or do anything that causes young people to lose sight) of the truth that they are profoundly loved by God and are a precious gift to the Church.

Gender identity

As gender expression is changing and diversifying, there is debate whether the traditional views of gender (God created humans male and female), which have been taught by churches throughout history, have a place in today's world. Before we engage young people in conversations about gender identity, it's helpful for us to reflect on our own inherited beliefs about gender and identity and to think about how we might hold space for young people to think about their developing identity.

Most of us were probably brought up with a traditional understanding of gender identity that goes something like this: a baby is assigned male or female at birth depending on their biological sex. One is (in most cases) either male or female and biology has the final say on the matter. Gender is a natural expression of your biological sex. If you are born female, you perform female in clearly defined ways (i.e. you're nurturing, sensitive, etc., or whatever expectations exist in your family/cultural background). If you're born male, you perform male in clearly defined ways (i.e. you're aggressive, assertive, decisive, etc., or whatever expectations exist in your family/cultural background). Failure to do so means you're deviating from what's agreed as normal behaviour – and that's not encouraged.

For years this view of gender identity was self-evident and, apart from lone voices in society, was largely unchallenged. But over the past fifty years there's been a move to separate gender from biological sex, enabling us to *challenge* the idea that not only certain behavioural traits of men and women but also the positions they hold in their family, immediate community, church or wider community, are natural expressions of their biological differences. Is being a leader a natural expression of what it means to be a man? Is being devoted to domestic affairs a natural expression of what it means to be a woman? Although biological sex might be fixed, what it means to be a male or a female are culturally conditioned and can vary greatly.

This may seem self-evident to us today, but this is still relatively new thinking. Up until the 1960s, the word 'gender' only appeared in relation to linguistic pronouns (*le/la* in French and *der/die/das* in German, for example). Gender was first applied to a person in 1968 by an American Professor of Psychiatry called Robert Stoller, because he wanted to make a distinction between biological characteristics and psychological ones. This paved the way for the idea that someone could have male biological characteristics (penis, testes, scrota, etc.) and female psychological characteristics at the same time, making it easier to understand why a person may feel their gender doesn't match their sex.

In more recent years there has been a deconstruction of gender itself. Are there only two gender expressions – male and female? What about people who don't align with either? Are gender categories needed at all? For young people who don't align with the sex they were assigned at birth, is their gender expression (or non-conforming behaviour) a more accurate expression of who they are?

With all this complexity, it's unsurprising that many of us may feel concern that young people who experience an incongruence between their biological sex and their gender identity are 'encouraged' to transition, socially, hormonally or surgically. The question of whether it's our biological sex or our gender identity that has the final say on who we are can provoke a lot of reactions and wildly varying views, both within and outside the Church.

At the heart of this raging debate are precious young people. The available evidence suggests that LGBT young people are more at risk of anxiety, depression, self-harm and suicide than heterosexual or cisgender (identify with the sex they're born with) young people.[11] In his book, *Embodied*, Preston Sprinkle talks about how:

> many trans* people, especially teenagers, have co-occurring mental health concerns, sometimes several, like anxiety, depression, and eating disorders. Trans* people also experience borderline personality disorder, schizophrenia, obsessive compulsive disorder (OCD), attention deficit hyperactive disorder (ADHD), and autism spectrum disorder at a higher rate than the general public . . . Are these mental health issues a cause, a result, or simply correlated with being trans*? Specialists are divided, and I'm unqualified to give an authoritative answer to this complex psychological question. What we can say with confidence is that there may be other mental health concerns intertwined with a person's trans* experience.[12]

Young people in our churches who are questioning their sexual identity and gender identity need our unconditional love and compassion as they work this out with support from professionals and a wider network.

As we hold space for young people who are experiencing incongruence between their internal sense of self (gender identity) and biological sex (sex identity), we can celebrate biological sex as a gift from God that doesn't come preloaded with specific cultural ideas of gender. Jesus broke the first-century gender 'rules' when he washed his disciples' feet, cried in public, paid attention to the concerns of women and made them the spokespeople for some of the most important things he taught. We break the gender 'rules' of our age when we choose to be more like Jesus and not whatever idea of masculinity or femininity is getting the greatest attention in culture. It's possible to celebrate biological differences *and* resist gender stereotypes that oppress people while celebrating the wonder of being made 'in the image of God . . . male and female' (Genesis 1.27, NIV).

Handling these tensions

It's because of the painful realities experienced by LGBT+ people that many Christian young people struggle to know how to connect a loving God with a church's view of sexual or gender identity that seems (and at times *is*) oppressive. In my research, although 47 per cent of the young people who responded said they felt the church *should* teach them about no sex before marriage, the majority felt that the church *shouldn't* teach that sex should be between one man and one woman (41 per cent said the church should be teaching Christian young people that sex should be between one man and one woman). Their responses to this question point to both a confusion as to what Scripture means about one-flesh sexual union and a desire to be loving and inclusive to LGBT+ people – a desire fuelled by their Christian identity.

> This is a hard one because biblically this is what it says, but also it says we should love, and we want to be a space open to all to have conversations, then I think it's important to talk about sex with inclusivity.

> I have no clue!! I think the church should provide more guidance on whether any relationship other than a heterosexual one is OK – with proper biblical teaching – I and so many of my friends are SO confused on this!

Whether it's about sexual attraction, masturbation, porn use or experiences of sexual activity, every year young people exit the Church or feel unable to keep following Jesus. I remember one young person telling me that she had left her church because 'they're more loyal to their doctrine than they are to their young people'. When I pressed her, it was clear she wasn't referring to any particular teaching. Her sadness was to do with the church failing to engage in conversations around gender and sex identity. At the time when she and her peers were asking their big identity questions about what it would mean to follow Jesus, the church was unable to hold space for their questions, leaving many of them feeling shamed, confused and convinced that church isn't a place for them to work this all out.

Safety net

All young people, whether they're exploring faith or not, need to be able to explore all facets of their identity while knowing a secure foundation. This firm foundation is their intrinsic value as people created, known and loved by God. This gives them a safety net as they ask the big questions, because no question, experience, opinion from another person, circumstance or change in their reality will in any way damage or reduce their worth. Young people who are *not* allowed to safely explore and test out different identities might be left with what Erikson refers to as 'role confusion', meaning they're never sure what they like or believe or who they are. This is a disaster for life and for discipleship.

So how can we help support young people's identify formation so that they can become all they're made to be?

1. Hold space

Developing a sense of self is an enormous task, one that young people may at times feel overwhelmed by. So first we need to accept how important it is for young people to explore and test different identities that might be expressed in all sorts of ways. Having leaders who aren't afraid of adolescent identity formation can be a huge relief for young people who are picking up vibes that how they're behaving or what they're thinking is being perceived as a problem. Accepting how crucial self-exploration is for a young person's identity formation isn't the same as saying that we can't bring helpful challenge when we see damaging behaviours emerging. But there's a vast difference between giving room for healthy identity exploration and loading unhelpful expectations and conditions on what's being expressed.

In this process of exploring who they are, young people may land on identities that are provisional, transitional or permanent. Holding an undefended space for young people means inviting them to lay down their weapons of attack and defence, to just 'be' and to discover that Jesus is absolutely with them and really likes them as they explore who they are. He's more equipped for this than anyone. He's not in some imaginary future waiting for them to work out who they are before he can work his purposes in and through them.

One of the key ways God is working his purpose in and through young people who look to him is by inspiring them with the courage and confidence to let his Spirit lead them through this time. Jesus knows the young people better than we do. He can pinpoint the specific moment in their development so he knows exactly what they need. We know this in theory, but often in practice we find it a whole lot harder to trust our young people to Jesus than to our own 'brilliant' ideas about who they are and what they need! I remember a sixteen-year-old telling me that, as he realized his internal sense of self didn't match his biological sex, he felt Jesus was closer to him than he had ever known. Initially, I was trying to get my head around what he was saying and what I needed to do. Then I began to ask myself if I needed to be able to define it to be able to hold space for him as *he* asked it. And not just asked it of himself, but asked it before the God and *to* the God who created him.

It's raining as I write this. Sheeting rain that drenches you to the skin the second you leave the house. If we were to see God's grace as a deluge like this, wouldn't we *stop* telling young people to metaphorically put their hoods up and get inside? We'd be pushing them out of the door, saying, 'Get into that! Get into God's downpour of love and grace and power! Ask God all your questions. Bring to God all your fears, mess, desires and struggles. I'm right here too, splashing around in this stuff, cheering you on as you discover you are loved, wanted and known by your Creator.'

2. Spot the culture stories

Second, we need to be aware of some of the key narratives in culture that are shaping young people's sense of self. This will help us to develop a robust theological reflection on the forces that are capturing young people's imaginations. The church is to be an interrogation of the oppression of people in any culture at any given time – whether that's around racial segregation, gender inequality, poverty, mental health or the purpose of human identity.

Many of the young people I serve talk about how their peers believe that we are nothing more than a bunch of atoms in a meaningless universe, with no obligation to anyone other than ourselves. This current cultural story says it's implausible to believe in God – and even if you do believe in God, it makes no difference to your life. So young people in our churches are having to find their identity in a world where the cultural struts that supported the story of Christianity have long since been removed. This is a culture that has rapidly moved away from belief in a God who might have anything to say about your life, your identity. The idea that we find ourselves because we're surrendered to God is almost impossible for our culture to accept. At best it sounds like strange self-actualization. At worst it sounds like the ultimate in delusional repression.

We need to pay attention to these emerging stories, because they are influencing how young people hear and engage with the invitation at the heart of Christianity to be found in Christ. Here are four cultural forces shaping the identity narrative in western youth culture.

Digital revolutions

As the first Wi-Fi-enabled generation, they are the most self-directed, with access in their pocket to most of the world's living humans and information. Living online also means close proximity to a universe of pornographies, the consumption of which has the power to rewire their brains and recalibrate their ideas about self-worth, connection and intimacy.

What young people consume has the power to consume them. Many studies have shown how accessing pornography can lead to users having a more risky and casual approach to sex[13] and can even encourage men to behave more sexually aggressively towards women.[14] It's little wonder that gender-based aggression and violence within youth culture is increasing, with the culture of 'nudes' being a case in point. Whether a young person's involvement in creating, sending or receiving nudes is experimental or aggravated,** the risks to that person's well-being are well documented. Sexting isn't gender neutral; girls are more negatively affected. But the boys aren't safe either. The most significant influence on a young person's understanding of consent is gender, specifically ideas around masculinity. What heterosexual boy gets 'man points' from his peers for respecting a girl when she says 'no' to sexual activity or sending nudes? This is

---

** Experimental are incidents involving the creation and sending of nudes and semi-nudes with no adult involvement, no apparent intent to harm or reckless misuse. Aggravated are incidents involving additional or abusive elements beyond the creation, sending or possession of nudes and semi-nudes. UK Council for Internet Safety, 2021.

all played out against a backdrop of violent, aggressive behaviour against girls and women, perpetrated by men holding some of the most powerful positions in the world today (and church), which seem to be consequence free.

Rise of the 'nones'

The single fastest-growing religious group of our time is those who tick the box next to the word 'none' on national surveys. This is the first post-Christian generation, no longer governed by an ideology of Judeo–Christian morality that has dominated western thinking for the past 1,500 years. For many, traditional religion is seen as a straitjacket that curtails any sense of personal freedom.

In this climate of hostility towards and ignorance about faith, Christian 'fundamental' youth are any teens who express conservative ideas about sexuality and purity. When it comes to sexual ethics, many Christian teens growing up in Christian homes are metaphorically ticking 'none' when it comes to buying in to the traditional or historic views of sex that every church youth group would have taught in the 1990s.

New puritanism

In the wake of the weakening of the Christian story in public, there's a cultural power play. In many ways, it feels like Generation Y (otherwise known as 'Millennials', those born between the early 1980s and the mid 1990s) defines tolerance as, 'I'll disagree with you on this issue, but I'll fight for your right to disagree with me,' and Generation Z (typically born between the mid 1990s and the mid 2000s) takes tolerance one step further, seeing all beliefs as equally valid. The challenge, though, is when people's beliefs clash – who is right? Particularly in the digital space and increasingly in universities, mass media and public life, believing something that offends someone else makes you wrong. The no-platforming/cancel culture is an example of the invisible censoring of ideas. This ideology war makes discussion and debate about ultimate reality and what it means to be human feel potentially dangerous. It also renders the idea that their church might hold a view that same-sex relationships are not supported by Scripture *and* yet still be welcoming of gay people increasingly impossible for members of Generation Z to accept.

Post-pandemic

What must it feel like to be growing up in a world that is only made safe by science? What are the big lessons that the emerging generations are drawing from the 2020–21 global pandemic? Is it a renewed sense of valuing life because we realize how fragile it is? Or is there an increased apathy towards God because, although we may have prayed for a vaccine, the public perception will be that humanity can solve its own problems? As I write, we are yet to see the impact of living through a global pandemic on young people's understanding of God's involvement in the world and significance in their lives.

3. Communicate better

Third, it's important that we as leaders have a growing understanding of what being a Christian means in our own lives. Critical reflection on who we are in Christ helps us articulate to young people the difference Jesus makes to our identity every moment of every day. In an increasingly secular age, young people grow into what it means to be a Christian, not because they've heard a talk at a big event but by exploring authentic patterns of Christian belief that enable them to meaningfully live out their identity as followers of Jesus. Their faith identity needs to equip them to live well in a world that wants to undermine that identity at every turn.

I find that immersing myself in Scripture, listening to the Spirit and practising my faith are vital in forming and strengthening my identity as a follower of Jesus. I believe that if we as leaders don't allow God to shape us, we have nothing new to offer young people in this area. All we end up doing is stirring the pot of what's already there. But if we are serving young people out of a deepening place of our own identity in God, then we are released to walk well with young people, bringing the right input, support and challenge when it's needed.

Many of the young people I know need to be constantly reminded that they are unconditionally loved by God. If they don't grasp this, everything they seek to do is sin-management – stuff to try to make God like them a little bit more. It's religious activity that leads to self-reliance rather than Christ-sufficiency. Our job is to point young people to the

God who loves them with an unquenchable, fierce, unconditional love. We mustn't put any of our conditions on the way God loves them, or add any clauses to who God says they are, whether those clauses pertain to their virginity, sexual attraction and experiences or their identity. Nothing we do achieves the identity we crave – except that we accept all that Jesus has done for us. We can say, 'I am who I am because of the grace of God. I am becoming who God made me to be because of the grace of God.' A weak view of salvation says that we are (in God's view) 'in' or 'out' of God's love and purposes depending on our thoughts or activity (mostly about sex) from one moment to the next. Let's be vigilant against this lie.

The truth of Christian identity is that, as we give ourselves to him, God gives himself entirely to us. The truth of our belovedness is the beautiful beginning – there's more life-bringing God reality to delve into. The truth is that if we stop at this point, we're being miserly with the good news. Scripture tells us that our identity as God's children is not something we achieve but something we receive, and it's an identity that is not only given but that is *grown into* (see John 1.12).

This understanding of identity puts us at odds with a culture hell bent on rampant individualism. It is because God loves us as we are that we are able to grow into who he says we are. When we become a Christian, we don't become better versions of ourselves; we become new people, new creations devoted to living out this new identity as co-heirs of the kingdom of God. If we're inviting young people to access this truth and live by it, we'd better provide a huge amount of support, inspiration and practical wisdom around how this works on a day-to-day level in a culture that just doesn't get it. We also need to extend to young people oceans of grace as they (like us) take a lifetime to work this identity in and live it out.

In light of all these cultural stories and identity influences, it's so reassuring to think that God has seen the journey of adolescence a billion, trillion times. He embraces young people in their identity formation. He has made it so that he would be found by them in their wrestling. Our task is to walk with young people as they look to God in the midst of this unique time for them. What takes centre stage in adolescence continues throughout the whole of life. Discovering who we are and growing into who we long to be is a lifelong process. Helping young people during adolescence to direct their deep questions towards the one who knows them best and to experience him as the foundation on which to build their lives is our God-given task.

There's no fear in God; we don't need to be afraid.

Outside in; inside out

Outside in

- What are the key narratives in your community about young people, both positive and negative?
- What is it about young people's identity exploration that causes you concern or gives you hope?
- How does your church communicate its concerns and hopes for young people's identity exploration? What are the key messages about their identity that young people receive from your church community?
- Not all young people are engaging with a faith identity. What impact does being in a faith community have on young people's ability to explore their identity? What are some of the additional challenges or opportunities they face?
- How are you theologically reflecting on sexual identity and gender identity? How could you deepen your own Christian understanding of what it means to be a human made in the image of God?

Inside out

- What form did your own 'who am I?' questions take?
- How are you still wrestling with your understanding of your identity? What wisdom, empathy and conviction do you have that you can draw on in your work with young people?
- What are your hopes for the young people you work with as they explore their identity?
- What might your church do differently to support young people in this stage of development (both young people in the church and those in the wider community)?

- Where do the conflicts lie for you in supporting young people in their identity formation?
- How are you resolving these in yourself? What wider conversations might you need to have with others?
- What support from you and the wider church do you consider young people need to develop a healthy sense of self?

3

Yes, no, maybe

She stood on the stairs, hands clenched and arms locked against her sides. Opening her mouth wide, she shouted out one long word that lasted her entire breath.

'NOOOOOOOOOOOOO!'

Determined to win this one, but not lose my cool, I fixed her with my 'firm but fair' look and levelled with her. 'It's bedtime. It's not standing-on-the-stairs-shouting-at-mummy time.' I was quite proud of my little bit of sass at this pre-bedtime showdown, so I continued, 'I'm going to close my eyes and count to three, and by the time I reach three you will be up those . . .'

Before I could finish the edict, my five-year-old stuck her hands on her hips and declared, 'Mummy, I said "no" and my "no" is enough!'

I was impressed. In one swift move she had asserted herself and made it abundantly clear that where a five-year-old has a will, there's a parent who invariably gets in the way!

'My "no" is enough.'

As I tucked her up in bed, I thought of the young people I knew and the ways they established their unspoken rules, sensing each other's awkwardness and recklessness. Could they boldly assert their choices, even if it meant social alienation or ridicule? Did they believe their 'no' was enough? Did they trust themselves to know when to say yes? Did they trust each other enough to know their decision would be respected, or would they need to trade certainty in for a shrug, just to fit in? I know I did, many times. I still do sometimes.

One of the questions I'm most regularly asked by youth workers is how they can best help young people make good decisions about sex. One email I received recently worded it like this:

The young people I work with are dealing with so much in the area of sex that I never had to face when I was their age. I want to help them make better decisions about it all, but where do I start?

I've spent many hours with young people, unpicking the consequences of decisions made. But I'm sure I'm not the only youth worker to admit that I don't always know what the young people I'm working with are thinking or doing when it comes to sex. It's interesting that, with all we don't know, we tend to believe that whatever decisions young people are making about sex, they're probably not very good ones!

Why is this?

Mainly it's because we can often see first-hand the crushing pressure so many young people are under to conform to certain codes of belief and practice around sex in youth culture. We see and we want to arm them not just to survive adolescence, but also to thrive and possibly even to lead. But it's not just about the external pressures they face. We also see first-hand how, on the whole, young people don't make decisions like we do, or at least like the adults we're trying to be. They're more likely to act on impulse, behave irrationally, misread or misinterpret situations and emotions, get involved in fights and struggle to assess risk or to change damaging behaviours.

With a more sensitive emotional system, young people are wired to seek greater rewards and new and stimulating experiences. Their curiosity and readiness to try new things and be all-in for something is one of the things that makes working among them so inspiring. Of course, there are many adults who behave like this too, but studies have shown that as the adolescent brain is significantly different from the adult brain, there is a direct impact on how young people make decisions.

The brain game

Children's brains have reached 90–95 per cent of their adult size by the time they're six years old, but before they reach maturity (are fully formed), their brain needs to go through massive reconstruction and remodelling, and this happens during adolescence. Starting from the back, any grey matter that hasn't been used in the thinking and processing part of the brain is 'pruned' away, making the neural pathways more effective.

As this 'use it or lose it' process moves across the brain, back to front, a huge remodelling takes place. Last to get the treatment is the pre-frontal cortex, the infamous decision-making part of the brain. During the teenage years, when this decision-making centre of the brain is underdeveloped, young people come to rely on a different part of the brain to help them make decisions: the amygdala, the centre of all the explosive stuff like emotions, motivations, impulses and instinct.

Imagine you've just acquired a 'fixer upper' property. The external walls, windows and roof are all intact, but as you step through the front door there's carnage all around: floorboards have been pulled up to allow for underfloor heating to be installed, the loo is out of action as the plumbing is being sorted and the whole place is being rewired. It's going to be awesome, but right now it's carnage. What will get you from a house that looks like a building site to a house that feels like a home are all those essential, mundane tasks of clearing out the old and putting in the new. The same rules apply to the teenage brain.

When it comes to making decisions about sex, are Christian leaders expecting too much from young people? In linking good (which is often code for 'grown-up') choices about sex with being serious about following Jesus, are we setting Christian young people up to fail? When I ask young people at church what they think about sex, I often get fairly standard statements like, 'You're not really supposed to do it until you're married,' or, 'God made it.' Sometimes, these are said with an upward inflection at the end, like it's a question. When I ask the same young people how they're making decisions about sex, I often get shrugs and silence. It might be because they don't want me to know, which is fair enough. But it's more likely that in asking them to describe their decision-making process, I've asked them something that their adolescent brains can't easily articulate.

Good decision-making is a life skill that takes a while to develop. As neurological changes during adolescence are putting the teenage brain under constant stress, young people's psychosocial immaturity means they're at greater risk of making choices on impulse and are more susceptible to be influenced by social rewards from peers. It should come as no surprise when young people make poor decisions. By preloading ideas like 'serious commitment to Jesus' with developed decision-making skills, we're in danger of adding to the stress the adolescent brain is under, making it more likely that a young person will make poor decisions about sex. In my experience, it's not always as simple as young people not 'knowing' what the right or most healthy thing to do might be. It's not even that they don't know what their parents or churches might believe about sex. It's just they're at the early stages of learning how to take what they know and turn it into what they *do*.

But as well as asking them to articulate a process they're not yet fluent in, I'm asking them to engage in a topic with high emotional stakes. Talking about sex can make young people feel anxious, curious, excited, disgusted, ashamed, angry or upset. The impact of this emotional arousal on their decision-making, twinned with their desire to follow Jesus ('I need to get this right to be a good Christian'), explains why Christian teenagers might be able to discuss with you why saving sex for marriage is a good idea, but then engage in premarital sexual activity when they're with peers online or in person.

The question for you and me is what we do with that.

The very worst thing would be to tell a young person that their actions are evidence that they're being rebellious or not serious about Jesus. Of course, none of us would say this. But unless we reflect on what's actually happening right now for this young person, we might find ourselves responding in unhelpful ways. When asked the worst thing churches can do for Christian young people in the area of sex, these were the most common responses in the survey:

Albeit with good intentions, but when churches create such a high bar, a perfect vision for their sex lives so that everyone feels a failure from the start and carries a guilt that erodes their confidence and self-worth.

To preach messages without any acknowledgement and compassion toward the fact that many young people have already sinned within this area. This will only turn them away from the church and will potentially give them lifelong feelings of shame and guilt.

These young people have an assumption that they will at some point make mistakes about sex. When they don't receive support and teaching on how to handle poor decision-making, they're unsure whether their church leaders or parents will be safe places to turn when they need help. If adolescence is a time when decisions are guided more by emotions and less by logic, wouldn't it be better for us to help them handle their emotions rather than encourage adherence to and performance of a certain set of choices that aren't yet owned by the young people? Our goal isn't to stop stuff happening, but to help young people when stuff does happen to connect their real experiences with a real Jesus who meets them in real situations. It's powerful for all of us to hear that we might not always make the right decision in any given situation, but that doesn't mean we're not able to pause, reflect and behave differently next time.

But in case you think the only way to help young people is to be there when it all goes wrong, think again. Acknowledging the unique role the adolescent brain plays in decision-making doesn't mean that we abandon young people to their stage of development and to other people's negative or damaging influence. Some of the choices around sex carry significant or lifelong consequences; we would be irresponsible and unloving if we didn't talk about how young people can protect themselves from situations that could lead to such consequences. As well as helping them to find grace when they make mistakes, our goal is to equip them to stand firm in who Jesus says they are, and one of the best ways to do this is to help set the boundaries for their safety and success.

So what sort of steer, guidance, input and support do young people need from us at this critical stage in their lives? Let's pay close attention to how they think about, anticipate, approach and experience decision-making so that we can help them not only make good choices in the moment but also grow in confidence and skill to develop healthy habits that will shape the pattern of their lives.

Invite curiosity

Humans are built to learn. We're hardwired for it and we learn best when we're curious. Researchers Nico Bunzeck and Emrah Düzel did an experiment in which they tested people with familiar and unusual images to see how their brains reacted to new things. There's a region in our midbrain called the SN/VTA that is the major 'novelty centre' of the brain, which responds to novel stimuli. Bunzeck and Düzel's experiment showed that only *completely new things* cause strong activity in the midbrain area.[1]

We know that young people are drawn to explore the unknown and to be more reckless with their curiosity, which is why warnings don't always work. Telling a youth group not to leave their dorms at night on the youth weekend away because 'the corridors between the girls' and the boys' dorms are being guarded by a patrol of killer badgers' tends to ensure everyone is wide awake all night trying to defy the vicious beasts and get into each other's bedrooms.

Young people's insatiable desire to know what's out of reach and to explore new limits is also instructive. When young people's curiosity is piqued, their brains enter a state where they are more readily able to explore and grasp something, and their desire to push boundaries means they're more likely to act courageously about their new discovery. When Rani heard her youth leader speak passionately about how unjust it is that people are living and dying without knowing Jesus, she immediately signed up to join the church's street evangelism team. At twelve, she was not only the youngest person to join the team, but she was also the boldest. What do you want the young people you disciple to be curious about?

I don't think you need much imagination in today's world to consider what a life of many sexual partners and experiences looks like. Those role models are everywhere: in films and song lyrics, played out on social media and evident in the lives of public figures. But what would it take to spark curiosity in young people for a life of sexual restraint? The deep belief that restraint isn't repression but the path to freedom is a powerful part of our understanding of what it means to be human, so it needs to be part of how we live our lives among young people – and what we're inviting them into. Choosing the discipline of abstinence (deciding why and where I will set my limits) creates spaces to develop the skills of engagement (deciding what I will say yes to and why). Affirming that a young person has the capacity and can grow in confidence to say no to non-consensual, unwanted, unplanned sex and intimate acts is something we should be aiming for. It's a privilege to invite young people to explore and experience chastity (as a rule of life outside marriage, or as a season of time) as an alternative path through the turmoil of adolescence; to be wild in their constraint, positive in their consent. 'No' isn't negative – it's relentlessly positive. 'When everything is possible, nothing is desirable . . . without the word "no" sexual fulfilment itself vanishes.'[2] I'm saying no to a sugary snack now so that I can say yes to the feast in an hour. I'm saying no to a porn-fuelled sex life so that I'm more likely to experience satisfying sexual intimacy in a real relationship throughout my life.

I appreciate that borders on idealistic. Too often, the church has presented a false horizon of perfect sex as a reward for chastity before marriage. I don't want to replace curiosity regarding the unrealistic aim of perfect sex with multiple partners with an unrealistic aim for a perfect partner if you don't have sex before marriage. Christian idealism is a dangerous ingredient when it comes to understanding our sexual decisions. There is no such thing as a perfect sexual partner guaranteed by God. There are satisfying sexual experiences, there are disappointing sexual experiences and there are damaging ones. These sexual experiences can happen in casual sexual encounters and can happen in 'Christian' marriages. Young people we work with will probably have experience of adult relationships in their lives that are healthy and those that are not. But the idea that our adolescent imagination doesn't have a role to play in shaping our decisions is misguided. What would it take for us to help young people get curious about *why* God asks us to order our sex lives along such radically different lines from those of wider culture? We're not about making young people's decisions for them, but we are about developing highly effective strategies to help them foster positive behaviours for life in today's world.

One of the most powerful ways of posing questions to young people is often to begin with the words, 'I wonder . . .' I wonder if there's a different way to do . . . I wonder if God has something to say about . . . I wonder what you're thinking would be the right decision to make.

Curiosity is a prophetic gift that helps us as leaders too. It enables us to navigate a clear path between a depressive view of adolescent sexual decision-making – 'If only we could go back to how it was before, when young people didn't have all these pressures on their identity and choices' – and an anxious view – 'If only we could keep hold of them until they're old enough to actually make responsible choices, then all would be well.' Curiosity enables us to ask questions about what God might be doing in the young people's lives, even as they wrestle with their choices and make mistakes.

Make choice plausible

As well as increasing young people's curiosity about the power of really owning their decisions, it's important that we help them with the nitty-gritty of actually making decisions.

Although we tend to use the words interchangeably, choice and decision are two different things. Choice is the art of being about to identify and then choose between the different options before you (considering the possible consequences and what freedoms you're prepared to sacrifice for other freedoms, etc.). A decision is the conclusion reached after making the choice between the options before you. As we've already seen, young people's ability to think through their options, make their choices, anticipate the consequences, perceive they have control to make their own choices and then own their decisions is a huge task that they need support in. Every time we create space for young people to pause and think things through, we're creating a plausibility shelter (a phrase coined by Nick Shepherd and quoted in a number of his talks) over them where they can safely try out some of the skills they will need to use in the heat of a moment. Young people learn from each other as they listen to each other's experiences and reflections on what they did or would do differently next time.

Chatting through real-life scenarios with young people and allowing them to 'try out' different choices is a powerful piece of experiential learning. Whether it's acting out scenarios or using a storyline from a film or a current television series, whenever we encourage young people to think through choices and consequences, their perception of control in any given situation increases.

It's fascinating to me how often God uses this technique to prepare people for the decisions they will need to face in the heart of a battle. Think about the dialogue between God and Moses at the burning bush, or between God and Gideon as he was hiding in a wine press (Exodus 3; Judges 6). I get the sense that God wasn't just handing out an order but engaging his people in a process of 'what if?' that would see them ready to stand their ground in front of a pharaoh or an oncoming army. In helping young people to actively engage in their own decision-making process, we're not only empowering them to come to a decision but we're also preparing them to engage well with information, teaching, wisdom, their own values and their growing beliefs about how they will come to their decisions. Young people who want to honour God with their actions need to know that this isn't about sussing out the church-approved answers. It's being curious about God's word, inviting the Holy Spirit to speak to them, listening to the voices and experiences of other Christians and then making choices that are in line with their identity and beliefs as followers of Jesus.

Empower reflective practices

When asked who they turn to for advice about relationships and sex, 65 per cent of the Christian young people who took part in the survey said they go first to their friends. Personal research and study via search engines came in second (38 per cent), and praying came third (36 per cent). Studying Scripture came in fifth, at 31 per cent. Although we may feel encouraged that this is fairly high in the list (out of a list of fourteen options), at 30 per cent it's still a lot lower than their friends at 65 per cent. This could point to a closed feedback loop as young people simply pass on the limited information or wisdom they have discovered. If these are activities done in social settings or any ideas discovered are shared with friends, it shows how young people not only seek their friends first but also possibly filter what they've found or been taught through the lens of their friends. Or it could be an example of theological reflection: 'I face a dilemma, so I listen to the experience of my friends, I listen to the voices and teaching in Scripture, I listen to the Holy Spirit, I do my own research and I draw my conclusions.'

Our job is to help young people to take multiple sources of information and to keep asking questions. To have a wide circle of council is vitally important. Young people who grow up in closed-off communities (including church communities) where they're not encouraged to listen to other voices may be more suspicious about information or wisdom that's outside what's familiar or approved. Helping young people know how to find good-quality information and to distinguish between the information and ideas on offer should be a focus of our conversation with young people.

Outside in; inside out

Outside in

- How have you seen young people approach their choices and decisions?
- What's your reflection on how a young person has engaged with what you've communicated with them about sex?
- Do the young people you serve sense that they have the power to control themselves in the situations in which they need to make decisions?
- Have you noticed a gap between how young people think they should make decisions and how they actually make decisions?
- What do you put this gap down to?

Inside out

- What sparks *your* curiosity about what the Bible teaches about human sexuality and sexual relationships?
- How are you spending time formulating your own questions and discovering answers to ensure that, rather than just presenting Bible verses as proof texts or closed statements, you're sparking curiosity in how young people engage with the Bible and Christian teaching on sex?
- What other voices, personal experiences and sources of information and wisdom help you in your own decision-making process?
- How could you help young people widen their council of reference to include wisdom and helpful information from voices both within their community and outside?
- How can you be creating more opportunities for young people to listen to God?
- How would you define a positive decision-making process?

4

Pubes, nudes and dudes

It was when I mentioned the word 'period' that the front row groaned. We're talking full-on disgust faces. Only a few, but I wasn't expecting this. I tried out some more. 'Wet dreams, pubic hair, masturbation. How about prolapsed anuses?' More groans and some sniggers. There was a definite sense that a number of people listening weren't 'gonna go there'.

So what would they be prepared to talk about with young people? Because this was a room of youth leaders. Mostly employed by churches. Good at their jobs. With a remit to walk with young people as they navigate life and find faith. So why was there a sense of revulsion from some of them to address the one thing absolutely intrinsic to the daily lived experience of every young person they would ever meet and serve? Why was puberty such a no-go area? After all, Jesus experienced it. As did Paul. Esther. Peter. Deborah. You. Me. You get the point. Puberty happens to us all. More than that, it's something to be marvelled at: the sheer amount of change that takes place during puberty is extraordinary. I remember hearing someone once comparing it to moving from a 1990s dial-up modem to high-speed fibre broadband, or like driving off a country road onto a motorway.

Sadly, the church has often been guilty of responding to puberty as an unwelcome age of sexual awareness that will inevitably lead to young people falling into sexual sin. We see children change overnight from 'innocent' children to gawky, hormonal, sexually curious teenagers and think, 'Yikes – they're about to know about sex and be interested in sex and possibly even have sex. This is really bad!' Whereas God looks over a young person going through puberty and says, 'Wow. This is inherently good.'

As well as puberty being good, it's challenging. At every stage of puberty, young people need support in understanding how their bodies are developing in readiness for sexual reproduction and what this means to them. Simply being capable of sexual reproduction (twinned with reaching an age where sexual activity between consenting peers is legal) doesn't indicate that young people are ready for sex, even if they're receiving pressure from peers and youth culture to start being sexually active. Young people need support from trusted adults and peers to help them see it's possible and preferable to understand and celebrate the changes happening in their bodies during puberty *without* being sexually active.

A positive and informed approach to puberty (with all the internal and external pressures around sex that young people face during these years) is core to our reimagination of conversations with young people about sex.

Puberty is good

Puberty is primarily about sexual maturity. It's the life stage where a child's body matures into an adult body capable of sexual reproduction. Puberty is kicked off by hormonal signals from the brain to the ovaries in girls and to the testes in boys, which then produce hormones that signal to the rest of the body a stimulation in growth in skin, hair, muscle, bones, blood, breasts and sex organs. It's described as the 'filling-in' of a child's body from girl to woman, from boy to man. It's an awe-inspiring, God-created transformation. Before puberty, the recognizable physical differences between girls and boys are the sex organs, known as the primary sexual characteristics. But puberty leads to the differences between female and males being more pronounced, as secondary sexual characteristics develop.

Professor James M. Tanner, a child development expert, identified five visible stages of puberty in girls and boys. Although each young person has a different puberty timetable, it's helpful to use these 'Tanner Stages' (better known as Sexual Maturity Ratings) to help us understand sexual development during adolescence and anticipate the information and support young people may need. However, no table or list replaces asking a young person what it's like for them and what they would like from you.

Table 1 outlines Tanner's five stages of puberty.[1]

Table 1 Tanner's five stages of puberty

		GIRLS	BOYS
Stage 1	No noticeable signs of change in girls' or boys' bodies, but the brain is beginning to send signals to the body to prepare for change.	This usually begins to happen after the eighth birthday.	This usually begins to happen after the ninth or tenth birthday.
Stage 2	The beginning of visible physical development as hormones begin to send signals to other parts of the body.	From age nine onwards, breasts appear under the nipples. Often called 'breast buds', they can be of different size from each other and can be itchy or tender. The darker area around the nipple begins to grow. The uterus begins to grow larger and pubic hair can begin to grow on the lips of her vagina.	From age ten onwards the testicles and scrotum begin to get larger and hair can grow at the base of his penis.
Stage 3	The physical signs of puberty are becoming more obvious.	Around the age of twelve, her pubic hair gets thicker and curlier, breasts buds grow larger, hips and thighs start to fill out, acne can appear on her face and back, hair begins to grow under her arms and there can be a surge in her height.	Around the age of thirteen, his penis gets longer and the testicles grow bigger, his voice may begin to 'crack', muscles grow larger, he may begin to have 'wet dreams' (night-time ejaculation when he's asleep) and there can be a surge in his height.
Stage 4	Full-on puberty.	Around age thirteen onwards, girls can start their period (although this can happen much earlier for some girls), pubic hair thickens and breasts pass the 'bud' stage.	Around age fourteen, acne can appear, armpit hair begins to grow, his voice deepens permanently, and his penis, testicles and scrotum grow longer and larger.
Stage 5	The stage that marks the end of puberty (sexual maturity).	Around age fifteen, her breasts reach their adult size, her reproductive organs are fully developed, there's more pubic hair across her inner thighs, she has fuller buttocks, hips and thighs and her period will begin to be more regular. Girls reach their adult height typically two to three years after their first period.	Around age sixteen, his penis and testicles have reached their adult size, facial hair grows, pubic hair will have filled in and spread to his inner thighs, and he will typically have reached his adult height by age eighteen.

Although there are, of course, exceptions to any list that seeks to classify people into defined sex categories, puberty is a potentially unsettling time physically and emotionally for any young person. Throw into the mix increased body odour, acne, involuntary erections, media portrayals of the perfect body, easy access to online porn, self-consciousness and a church that might struggle to talk about any and all of it, and you've got a recipe for a few challenging years. For some young people, their body changing in ways that don't necessarily match their gender identity can be immensely distressing. Make sure you're listening well to young people with more complex needs and are signposting them and their families to appropriate groups for more specialized support. Remind every young person that there's no one way to feel about pubertal development. More than anything, they need to know this is a safe place for them to journey through puberty, however that looks for them.

Approached positively and handled well, puberty offers us opportunities to support young people at the beginning of their sexual maturity and allows us to create with them a positive and safe culture for ongoing conversations about sex. Puberty preparation isn't an add-on; it's a core dimension of our youth ministry.

Power in the mention

When I took over leading a younger youth group at church, I encouraged us to create a culture of mentioning things. As a team of youth work volunteers, we asked ourselves what it meant that we were discipling young people aged ten to twelve who were already experiencing puberty. What might they need from us in the way of information and support? What would we need to 'mention' to indicate that we wouldn't shy away from anything they were facing? One of our ideas was to regularly stick words up on a white board or around the room. These words didn't necessarily lead to big discussions but were signals to the young people that this was a space where everything could be talked about – nothing was taboo or off limits. I remember one Sunday grabbing the flip chart paper and announcing that Jesus was a teenager and totally gets the whole puberty thing so let's mention all the stuff anyone going through puberty might hear about, have questions about, or think is scary or funny. We wrote down loads of words. Some young people didn't speak. Others had loads to say.

One boy in the group had anxiety about puberty, fearing that the physical changes would be too much for him to handle, so a male leader spent some time the week before chatting it all through with him so he was aware, prepared and comfortable about what was going to happen in the session.

We'd fling questions out there like, 'How did Jesus deal with zits or bad body odour?' and, 'Do you think Jesus was friends with girls?' These didn't always get a response there and then, but it was our hope that these young people would grow to understand that the whole of us is contained within God – that's our genitals and hormones as much as our heart and mind. We sensitively and confidently mentioned words young people wouldn't normally associate with church so that they would be less inclined to believe that God was squeamish about their puberty.

If we were to create a 'power in the mention' list for what the Christian community would need to talk about to prepare young people well for puberty, what would it include? Here are some things to get us started: acne, public and private behaviour, body odours, vagina, menstrual cycle, wet dreams, hymen, desire, ejaculation, height and weight, emotions, periods, female body image, vulva, facial hair, mental health, penis, feeling self-conscious, testes, sleep, male body image, online porn, foreskin, secrecy, masturbation, vaginal opening, labia, pubic hair, personal hygiene, masturbation hygiene, friendships, peer pressure, clitoris . . . The list goes on.

Of course, we don't need to be medical experts to be able to support young people during puberty, but a working knowledge of the key changes in their bodies is really helpful. If puberty is primarily about sexual maturity, then helping young people frame what's happening and process this is crucial. Sex education is never just about bodily functions, infections and reproduction. It's also about the development of values, attitudes and beliefs that underpin how they live and build relationships throughout the whole of their lives. But helping a young person begin by putting their experience of puberty into a wider context of their body being a good gift from God helps to form in them an understanding that their capacity for sexual feelings and sexual activity is also a good gift from God.

Although speaking of a different good thing created by God, Paul writes to young Timothy that 'God doesn't want us to be shy with his gifts, but bold and loving and sensible' (2 Timothy 1.7). I don't think it's too big a leap to say that because puberty is created by God, he wants us to be equipped to handle it in healthy, honouring ways.

So how might we want to reimagine conversations with young people about puberty?

Is it OK?

Young people may feel unsure or insecure about all these physical changes they're experiencing. It's important that, as safe and trusted adults, we challenge misinformation and myths about bodies ('all girls have big boobs', 'boys should be taller than girls', 'you get acne because you're dirty') and reassure young people that what they're going through is part of the natural process of sexual development. None of this puts them at odds with their developing faith identity or their acceptance in the church. This may seem obvious to us, on the other side of puberty, but when this is the first time you're experiencing in your body the rush of powerful hormones that are activating growth in your genitals and reproductive organs, it can feel like 'the flesh' is in charge.

In times like these, young people growing up in church are most vulnerable to internalizing suggestions that their body is bad and only their spiritual life is pleasing to God. But Jesus is concerned for young people's body hygiene (regularly showering, confident use of menstrual products, washing hands after going to the toilet, etc.) as well as their spiritual hygiene (saying sorry and being forgiven, bringing their cares to God, setting boundaries to limit or prevent access to online sexual images and porn, etc.). When we teach and model the integration of both, we are helping young people to accept their bodies as good and know that they can make positive choices about them.

Make lots of time for the M words

First, let's talk about the menstrual cycle – and this is *not* just a section for female readers. The menstrual cycle refers to the monthly hormone cycle in the female reproductive system as her body prepares for pregnancy. The cycle begins with the first day of the woman's period and goes through to the first day of her next period. It lasts around a month (some women have longer or shorter cycles) and her period will last anywhere from two to seven days. In that time, she will lose between 30ml and 40ml of blood, which comes from the shedding of lining of the uterus (womb) if the egg isn't fertilized. The most fertile point of the cycle is when the egg is released, which usually happens between eleven and sixteen days before the woman's next period is due. This cycle is repeated every month until a woman reaches menopause.

A girl will usually begin her menstrual cycle around a year after getting a white vaginal discharge that she might see on her knickers or two years after her breasts start to develop. For the first few years after her period starts, they might not be regular, but from the moment she begins her periods (and in the days prior to her first period) a girl could get pregnant.

Being prepared with knowledge and support makes all the difference for girls as they begin their menstrual cycles. They need to know about different menstrual products (sanitary towels, tampons, menstrual cups, etc.) and how to use them. They also need support to know how to deal with the emotional and physical symptoms that can happen before or during her period (often referred to as PMS – premenstrual syndrome).

Even though I had been told about periods, I still believed the strange notion that my first period would be heralded by a piece of string hanging out of my vagina. I had obviously misunderstood what I had heard about tampons! I remember avidly checking myself every day from around my twelfth birthday to see if the string had appeared. Notwithstanding this false start, I generally felt positive about having a body that bled once a month.

When I reached my late teens/early twenties, I met a group of Christian peers at Bible college who were pretty squeamish about periods. Some of the guys would even jokingly say that the reason women couldn't lead men in church was because their monthly periods made them unclean and unhinged. I had never come across this before and it shocked me that the natural rhythm of my body was something these young men felt entitled to objectify and criticize. For many girls, this belief that their bodies are bad can start with a lack of education and support around understanding their menstrual cycle.

Years later, I worked at a youth club on a housing estate in North London. Some men on the estate were asking young teenage girls to give them blow jobs in the play park after school. The men were arrested, and our team began to support the girls. One week we took them on a residential, and in the middle of the night shrill screams woke everyone up. One girl had gone to the toilet and found a drop of someone else's period blood on the toilet seat. All the girls began a witch hunt as to who it might have been. 'Are you on your period?' they accused each other. Girls were crying, some were shouting; they were feeling anger and shame, and it didn't take a genius to realize it wasn't really about the blood on the toilet seat.

A few days later, I sat with them and drew a picture of the female reproductive system. They couldn't really name any of it and they were angry with me for using the correct names.

'You're making us watch porn,' one of them muttered.

'This is your body,' I said, as I continued to explain the different parts of their bodies. These thirteen- and fourteen-year-old girls were stunned. They sat watching intently.

'Porn doesn't help us understand how fabulous and unique our bodies are,' I reminded them. 'All this is inside you. It's yours. No one has the right to touch you. No one has the right to tell you you've got a fishy fanny or you're a dirty bleeder or you should shave your vagina or should show them your bits (I was quoting back at the girls things they had been told about their bodies). This is *your* body. It's amazing. You need to know how it works so that you can love, protect and care for it.'

In recent years, campaigns to end period poverty have brought to light the injustice of poor access to menstrual products, health care and education faced by millions of girls and women around the world. One report in 2019 said that one in ten girls in the UK is unable to afford menstrual products, resulting in detriment to her self-esteem, education and overall quality of life. A staggering one in five girls has reported being a victim of bullying and teasing because of her periods.[2] It's a reminder that girls are still growing up in a world that sees their bodies as a problem. The stats are heartbreaking: 80 per cent of British girls and young women have considered changing something about their appearance and 39 per cent said they feel upset because they can't look the way people do online;

51 per cent of girls aged seven to ten say they believe women are judged more on what they look like than what they do.[3]

This evidence points to a need for us to understand and identify whether aspects of girls' experiences during puberty are tied to higher rates of emotional difficulties.[4] Creating the environment for girls to process the changes happening in their bodies during puberty and the impact on their emotional well-being is essential to seeing girls flourish into embodied, confident young people.

But it's not just girls who benefit from body positivity education. In an age where porn educates many attitudes to sexuality and bodies, it's vital that all young people can understand the changes in male and female bodies in the context of getting ready for life as adults and all that can go with that: interacting with colleagues at work, having intimate relationships, becoming parents, remaining sexually faithful to someone, caring for the environment. Porn shows young people body parts and penetration; it doesn't teach them about healthy sexuality. It doesn't prepare them for life as healthy, fulfilled, self-controlled, sexual human beings.

More on porn later. But first let's talk about the other M word.

The other M Word

There is no other sexual behaviour so indigenous to the human species, more thoroughly discussed, more roundly condemned, yet more universally practiced than masturbation.[5]

For many Christians, masturbation is one of the most contested areas in adolescent sexual development. Is masturbation normal? Is it healthy? What's the difference between the odd 'wank' and habitual self-pleasuring? Is it possible to do it and not sin?

During puberty, young people's bodies are going through huge hormonal upheavals – which is what God designed for them to do. As young people's bodies mature, they may experience orgasms during the night owing to dreams that may or may not be erotic (and over which they have no control). These are referred to as 'wet dreams' because when young people have these kinds of dreams, they may wake up with wet bedding owing to (boys) emission of semen because they ejaculated or (girls) vaginal wetness.

As young people become more sexually aware, they may begin to explore their bodies, which often includes masturbation. Touching and rubbing their own genitals for sexual pleasure, which might or might not end in them having an orgasm, can serve as a relief for these new sexual feelings. It's also enjoyable because God created our bodies with the capacity to experience sexual pleasure. Discovering this in the privacy of their own room or a locked bathroom, in the secrets of their own body, is a huge deal. This sort of solo exploration during puberty is good as part of the bigger goal of understanding their God-given capacity to experience sexual desire and pleasure. These early sexual explorations are also moments where ideas about personal responsibility, privacy, setting boundaries, self-care and the possibility of exercising self-control can begin to take shape.

By telling young people that touching themselves sexually is automatically sinful behaviour, we're far less likely to engage them in healthy, godly conversations about it. A way into these conversations is to explore basic masturbation hygiene: why it's good to wash their hands after masturbating and to throw away any tissues they've used. Why it's not OK to masturbate in bed at night if they're sharing a bedroom with a sibling. How it's against the law for under-18s to share footage of themselves masturbating or for anyone to ask to watch them doing it on video call or online. How doing it a few times every day can affect what else they might want to be or could be doing.

Having a safe adult to process all these issues with increases the possibility that young people will perceive that they can make choices about how much it happens, when it happens and how it happens.

Let me pause here.

It can feel incredibly uncomfortable to be talking this way about young people's sexual development. More than anything, we want young people to be free from obsessive thoughts and habits around all sexual activity. We want them to be free from the harm that sexual sin causes. Hearing someone say that it's good for youth leaders to talk with young people about locking the bathroom door when they masturbate so their younger siblings don't walk in on them can seem like we're encouraging them to lose their innocence or to develop habits that are unhelpful, even sinful. But let's interrogate that idea further.

As a teenager, I thought that all and every kind of touching myself to feel sexual pleasure was inherently wrong, and when I first began working with young people, I passed on that belief to them. As a young person, I was confused by how much I enjoyed masturbating and by how deeply shameful it made me feel afterwards. Each time I did it, I thought I was further betraying my future husband, damaging myself and disappointing God. Sometimes, I dreaded being alone in my room in case I did something 'horrible' (i.e., masturbate). Unsurprisingly, I came to think of myself as horrible. I felt so bad, the only thing that helped was to masturbate.

This early confusion took years to resolve. The connection I felt with my body through using masturbation to deal with my self-disgust and shame nurtured in me false ideas about my body and about sex. I began to see sexual pleasure as something I wasn't allowed to have, something wrong and dirty. Over the years, I've discovered that I'm not the only person to have internalized a deep sadness over my struggles with masturbation.

A masturbation habit that's tied in with unmet needs and is allowed to develop without being spoken about, fuelled by sexual fantasy and graphic materials, does nothing helpful to a young person's sexual development. In fact, it can be hugely damaging, but this can be prevented. For the vast majority of people, the very first steps taken on the journey towards sexual maturity begin alone, in private and in uncertainty, so dropping 'sin' over it all can cause immense damage and lead to secrecy, driving young people away from the godly and wise conversations they need to access at this important time in their lives and towards dehumanizing sexual content that wants to educate and 'satisfy' them. Referring to masturbation as sin per se is an assumption from silence in the Bible – it just isn't ever talked about.

We need to think carefully about why we're so keen for young people *not* to masturbate. If we are saying to Christian young people that as well as holding back from sex before marriage, they need to avoid masturbation, we've got to know why. I've heard it said in many church circles that masturbation is dishonouring your future spouse. But do we really believe that? Do the actions of a young person who is exploring their sexuality during adolescence amount to wilful dishonouring of a future spouse? When a young person finds relief in sexually stimulating themselves once a day during their teenage years, are they acting in disobedience against God?

What's the deal with Onan?

The Bible never speaks against this sort of self-exploration or against masturbation itself. In his book *Understanding Adolescence*, Dr Roger Hurding asserts that 'the scriptures can be searched from cover to cover and no incident or statement can be found which forbids "solo-sex"'.[6] When you think of the range of sexual situations and practices mentioned in Scripture – erotica, rape, bestiality, sex for procreation, incest, men having sex with men, women having sex with women, prostitution and adultery – it's surprising that masturbation isn't mentioned at all. The sin of Onan in Genesis 38.8–10 (for years used as a proof text against masturbation) was nothing to do with solo sex. It was God's judgement against a man who refused to fulfil his duty before God to impregnate his dead brother's wife – which is yet again another tricky passage to understand in today's context – but it's not about masturbation.

There's another argument against masturbation that says that Jesus never masturbated so neither should we. This teaching runs with the idea that if Jesus was tempted in every way but without sin, and if he only did what he saw Father God doing (John 5.19), then how could we ever think that Jesus masturbated? It would mean that he would have seen the Father masturbating. Jesus' sexuality is important to consider, but this line of logic conflates all forms of self-touching, sexual exploration and solo sex and sees them *all* as inherently disobedient, sinful behaviour. There's no doubt that Jesus' single status challenges the idea that our sexuality is simply about what we get up to behind closed doors. His chastity reminds us that the goal of sexual maturity isn't just marriage and having sex and babies. It's much bigger.

Just as sex is the joining of your body to another person, through faith and baptism, we become part of the body of Christ. Jesus' sexuality wasn't on hold because he never married – to say that would be to suggest that he was not fully human. In fact, his singleness is one of the lenses through which we understand what radical dependence on the Father looks like.

But his experience of puberty would have been real; he would have grown in awareness of his capacity for sexual pleasure and sexual connectedness because this is an essential dimension of maturing into adulthood. We don't know how he handled this. We're not sure if the culture of the day saw adolescent masturbation as part and parcel of growing up and didn't worry about it. We can be sure that, as his awareness grew, his desire to order his sexuality in ways that would honour the creation design for human sexuality would have grown. I have no doubt he would have stood out among his peers as a well-grounded, embodied, vibrant, engaged, compassionate young man. The only record we have of adolescent Jesus sees him hanging out at the Temple, teaching with breathtaking wisdom and insight. His mum (once she and Joseph had tracked him down) saw what was unfurling in her son, so she kept a loving eye on him, watching over him as he grew. 'His mother held these things dearly, deep within herself. And Jesus matured, growing up in both body and spirit, blessed by both God and people' (Luke 2.52).

A better way

Saying that masturbation is sin doesn't resolve the issue for young people who are navigating sudden sexual feelings and curiosities while also seeking to grow in their Christian faith identity. Over time, I found safe and wise people to talk to, who helped me learn to appreciate my capacity for sexual pleasure, to reset my thinking about my body and longing for intimacy *and* to set personal boundaries to help me honour God's purposes for my sexuality. But that journey has taken time – lots of it. Being prepared to have pragmatic conversations about masturbation equips young people to recognize where they are developing damaging sexual practices, to develop new beliefs and practices that increase their sense of self-worth, and to help them develop distraction, delay and refusal skills.

As masturbation has the potential to shape young people's sexual responses in their formative years, we need to be able to find ways to talk about it with them. But rather than tell them not to do it at all, I think a better approach is to consider *when* masturbation can become unhealthy or lead them into sinful behaviour? If we make this the focus of our conversations, then it opens up the possibilities of helping young people identify where sexual self-exploration or masturbation is shaping unhealthy sexual responses in them, and to know what to do about it.

What might these unhealthy behaviours be? It could be when a young person is relying on masturbation to meet their deeper need for status, control or power. It could be when they use it for emotional regulation – as a way to make themselves feel good. It could be when masturbation is being fuelled by external and escalating porn, erotic literature or sexual fantasies. It could be when young people are using it as a way to withdraw from the world and not face their problems or struggles. It could be when a young person is asking or forcing another young person to masturbate or to perform sexual fantasies with him or her.

The opposite of this could be sexual exploration or masturbation that young people do alone, in private and without using online porn or graphic sexual images to stimulate arousal. It could be young people masturbating once a day, or a few times a week, rather than a few times every day to the point where it affects their everyday activities. It could be where young people learn to spot the triggers that make it very difficult not to masturbate to porn (alone in their bedroom with their smartphone) so they can set some boundaries. They could share these with a trusted adult so that when they transgress these boundaries, they don't internalize shame, and when they manage to stick to them, they celebrate!

All of us are exposed to sexual stimuli every day: we pass an attractive person on the street; we see a billboard using semi-nudity to sell a product; we watch a film with a sex scene. As we mature, we learn how to cope with our own sexual arousal. We learn what we need to switch off or walk away from to help us manage our sexual responses. We might use sport, music, hobbies, sexual intimacy with a spouse, masturbation, the arts or times of worshipping God as ways to express our sexuality. We also learn that just because we feel turned on doesn't mean we need to stimulate ourselves sexually. We can delay or decide not to act on sexual feelings. Instead of being unhealthy, this is incredibly positive. Ideally, we want to achieve a balance between suppressing all responses and being at the mercy of all sexual stimuli.

This is the trajectory we want young people to be on. Some young people will find this easier than others. You may be chatting with young people who have never felt inclined to touch themselves sexually or masturbate during their teenage years. It's important that they don't feel under pressure to start. There are messages in society today that tell young people they should be exploring sexual activity (solo or with others) to find out about their sexuality. When young people are pushed into self-exploration that they're not ready for, it can lead to greater distress and confusion. But as response to sexual stimuli (visual and other) is strongest during adolescence, there will be young people in our church or family who will need non-judgemental, wise support to work out how to cope with their sexual responses.

Masturbation would be an important thing to talk about with young people even without the availability and amount of online pornographies and sexually explicit material, but this reality makes it even more pressing.

Power of porn

Pornography brings illegitimate counterfeit satisfaction for that legitimate longing to feel good and alive. It captivates us and gives us a false sense of 'aliveness'.[7]

When online pornography provides the backdrop to this generation's learning about sex and sexuality, it becomes less about 'if' and more about 'when' a young person will encounter ideas, values and images that run counter to God's purposes for our sexuality. The power of porn to shape and recalibrate young people's ideas about sex, sexuality and relationships is off the scale. We ignore it at our young people's peril.

For a teenager suddenly awoken to the world of sexual stimulation, the new sensations can be overwhelming. The teenage years are often linked to a period of experimenting with drugs, legal or illegal, but the world of online pornography presents them with a hormone high that is free and available whenever they find themselves with a smartphone – which, for most young people, is most of the time. Male and female libidos have often been compared to gas rings (guys) and slow cookers (girls) – guys are immediately stimulated by sexy images whereas girls take longer to get 'turned on'. The high level of availability and accessibility of porn renders these distinctions moot. Both sexes carry around the equivalent of an Amazon warehouse full of porn on their smartphones – stimulation is only ever a moment away.

Think about that for a second. This is no longer the world of wearing shades and donning a scarf even in summer in order to pop down to your newsagent to buy *Playboy*. This is the world where the potential for porn obsession is only a few clicks away.

Porn usage releases a powerful chemical into the body, called dopamine. It's one of the natural chemicals that steers us towards doing things that feel good. Sport releases dopamine, as does a good laugh with your friends, drawing a picture and dancing. The problem is that this inner reward centre in our brain can be hijacked by things that give us big surges of dopamine. Every time we watch porn, our brain floods with dopamine, so we want to do it again. We do it again, but now we need a greater fix of dopamine to reach the same 'high', so we begin to search for new images.

Online porn is not good for young people's sexual development. There is some good research into its impact on young people's brains and sexual development, and evidence-based approaches to helping young people who are developing addictive behaviours around porn use and masturbation. It's important we make the most of the resources on offer (see Appendix 3 for some ideas). Take the time to gen up on what will equip you to have conversations about porn and masturbation that will really help young people discern how to be wise in what they think and look at.

Navigating a minefield

So herein lies the pertinent question: how do young people masturbate without stimulating themselves through graphic or overt sexual images? Even if young people avoid watching porn or reading erotic literature, what is the role of sexual fantasies in their healthy sexual development?

Sexual fantasies will always be part of the human experience of masturbation. Our mind plays a powerful role in our experience of sexual desire, which is how God created it. It's impossible to desire sex without our minds getting involved. It's totally counter-intuitive to suggest to young people that the only masturbation that isn't sinful is when they're not thinking about anything sexual. If that's the case, then we need to think well about what makes for good, healthy, God-honouring sexual thoughts and fantasies. We need to be real about the thoughts and fantasies we feed, nurture and use that lead us away from good, healthy, God-honouring sexual thoughts and fantasies.

Fantasies are far better to be generated by the mind. The question is whether *all* sexual images in our mind will automatically lead us to want more-sexualized images. If young people are masturbating once a day using images in their minds of attractive people or the underwear section of a magazine, these images will sustain them. But if they are masturbating three, four, five or more times a day, these images in their minds or in the underwear section of a magazine will not sustain them. They will need to find more-sexualized images; then it is like a slippery slope.

You may be shouting at me, 'Hey, here's an idea. How about being told they don't need to masturbate at all?'

Yes, that's true. No one *has* to masturbate. No one *needs* to masturbate. But saying you can be free not to masturbate is very different from being told that you mustn't. Imagine a young person discovering that they can speak with someone about how to spot the difference between a sexual thought that is part of a heathy view of sex and a sexual thought that is part of an unhealthy view of sex. There's a huge difference between a young person thinking about someone attractive when they masturbate and a young person calling to mind scenarios of sexual violence and harm.

Power of fasting

Years ago, a friend set up an amazing online movement of male Christian students who were offering a strong bond of accountability to each other to stop masturbating because they wanted to take charge of their sexual thoughts and sex lives. It grew like wildfire. From conversations with a number of the guys who took part, it was obvious that, in a world of sexual unrestraint, these groups provided a much-needed, radical, life-bringing alternative. It was like finding water in a desert. In delaying or avoiding masturbation, they were discovering what it meant for them to exercise their sexuality in powerful and chaste ways that made them healthier men and potential partners.

I'm an advocate of movements like these to offer support for women and men. As young people enter early adulthood and have greater capacity to assess risk and exercise greater self-restraint, they need role models like these young adults, who are slightly ahead of them on the journey, demonstrating positive ways to order their sex lives. Periods of fasting from masturbation can open up vital spaces for reminding ourselves of our dependency on God. Seasons of fasting from masturbation can prevent it from becoming for a young person 'obsessive (preoccupation with sexual fantasies) and compulsive (one's masturbating habits become highly ritualised)'.[8] We want to support and equip young people to enter adulthood with appreciation of their capacity for sexual pleasure and awareness that they can place life-bringing limits on their sexual behaviours.

Masturbation will always be a shadow of the intimacy of two hearts, two minds and two bodies in a one-flesh union. But, as part of the greater design, seeing the role that sexual self-exploration and release can play in helping young people understand their sexual selves can liberate them from internalizing damaging ideas about sex, bodies and arousal. If we were less concerned with whether young people are masturbating and more concerned with helping them navigate their way around damaging guilt and self-loathing, maybe we would see more Christian young people enter their adult lives and relationships with a godly, healthy approach to sex.

Imagine being a Christian teenager today. Your body is changing. Your peers in church and at school are experimenting with online porn, boasting about wank-a-thons, pushing the red line of 'how far is too far?' Sometimes, you have such powerful sex dreams at night that you wake up wet, confused, still aroused. You've started finding ways to relieve the sexual build-up. It all feels so new and messy. Shameful. When you think about God, you feel a dread that somehow this all disgusts him. Imagine hearing a trusted adult at church say that it's not the worst thing in the world if you start masturbating. You hear them say things like, 'You can be free from obsessive and damaging sexual habits,' which you don't really understand, but you get the sense *they* know and aren't disgusted or disapproving of what's happening. You begin to hope that conversations with them about these new feelings and urges might be what you need – at least, not as bad as working it out on your own. You begin to chat one-to-one with a youth volunteer.

It takes ages to finally say what's up, but by the time you do you've heard them say enough real stuff to know that they won't be shocked or disgusted. And you get the feeling that they feel a bit awkward about it too, so they won't be too enthusiastic to chat about your sex stuff – because that would be weird!

When puberty preparation is missed within the life of the church, young people are left alone to navigate sexual development in a world of wall-to-wall sexualized images and in a youth culture that isn't geared towards their sexual well-being. Puberty is a time of great promise and possibility for young people. So, as adults who want to do the best we can at preparing and walking young people through puberty, let's pray that these years of development into sexual maturity will be a time when young people experience and begin to express God's hope for them to live sexually whole lives.

Outside in; inside out

Outside in

- What further research into the impact of online porn on young people's brains and sexual development do you think you would benefit from?
- What are the myths or ideas about puberty in your family/church/community?
- What do you feel is helpful and what do you feel is unhelpful about this?
- How do the young people you know feel about the onset of puberty?
- What have you been taught about masturbation? Do you agree?
- How will you ensure that, whatever your view on masturbation, the young people you work with know you are a safe person to talk to about their experiences and questions?
- Have you seen good examples of puberty preparation for young people, youth workers and parents?
- What might you want to reflect on in your own experiences of puberty and sexual development, to equip you to have positive conversations with young people about puberty?

Inside out

- What culture would you like to see your church create around the onset of puberty?
- What do the girls you serve need to hear about puberty and their sexual development?
- What do the boys you serve need to hear about puberty and their sexual development?
- If you're working with young people who are questioning their gender, how will you support them? It is important they know they are valued and welcomed in the church and youth group as they navigate the additional struggles and concerns that their bodies developing during puberty will raise for them.
- What meaningful rites of passage could help young people acknowledge and celebrate their progress through puberty? Make sure you engage young people in helping create these!
- What do you consider to be healthy for a young person to do in simulating themselves (i.e., they won't watch porn, but is it all right to think about someone they fancy? If this isn't a good idea, why not? What is it acceptable for them to be thinking about?)
- How would a young person know that you would be willing to have these sorts of conversations with them?

5

The Disney gospel

So far, we've looked at how young people develop their sense of self, their interactions with cultural narratives around sex, the role that the adolescent brain has on their actions and how they process their choices, and the upheaval of puberty. Now I want to look at how our understanding and presentation of the gospel shapes our conversations with young people about sex, especially those exploring a Christian faith identity.

Zeitgeist

There are two main reasons why I love the Disney film *Frozen II* – Olaf and Kristoff. Created from Elsa's magical powers, Olaf is the huggable, philosophical snowman I'd like to employ as our children's pastor at church. Then there's Kristoff, the kind-hearted boyfriend who at one point in the film is reunited with Anna after she's been out rescuing her sister, Elsa. Anna apologizes for going into the fight alone. Instead of displaying a bruised ego or expressing jealousy, Kristoff says, 'It's OK. My love is not fragile.' Even though Disney heroes come as simplified, sentimentalized, idealized versions of reality, Kristoff is, without doubt, the best of the bunch.

But Disney is often one of the best at sensing the zeitgeist. There's an amazing song sung by Elsa that speaks directly into this cultural moment. Although there's peace in her kingdom, Elsa is unsettled by her powers, so when a mysterious female voice, which only she can hear, begins to call out to her, she sets off across the sea to find her destiny – and the destiny she finds is none other than herself. Out of the walls of the ice palace, her mother sings to her, encouraging her that it is Elsa herself who has the power to make her dreams come true.

The message is clear: your life revolves around you. That doesn't mean you can't be kind or courageous, but these virtues ultimately serve to help you discover who you are. True bravery is embarking on the quest of self-discovery. This, in a nutshell, is the cult of the individual, a self-made identity where we feel entitled to have lives centred on ourselves, where everything we think or feel has the right to be expressed without restraint. Of course, that sounds amazing to an emerging generation growing up in a world tearing itself apart with injustice, oppression, poverty and suffering. If I can forge my own freedom based on doing what makes me happy, then I don't need to rely on any broken system or person to make that happen.

But how does this understanding of the individual affect how we present the gospel to young people, and what impact does individualism have on our conversations about sex?

Muddy mystery

After a seminar I had led in a marquee at a Christian youth festival, an older teenage girl came to find me. She was in floods of tears. 'Jesus wants me to be happy,' she sobbed, 'so why would he want me to stop having sex with my boyfriend?' She felt God was asking too much of her. In acting like a cosmic sex-cop, God, in her view, was forcing her to choose between loving him and loving her boyfriend. How could he do that? Why would she want to believe in a God who did things like that?

My heart went out to her as she wrestled with how to process what this all meant for her. I could only agree with her that if the best Jesus had for her was for her to be happy, then he'd be a pretty rubbish divinity if he stopped her doing the things that made her happy. She paused. Then we found a dry corner in the muddy field and kept chatting.

This conversation has resonances with what sociologists Christian Smith and Melina Lundquist Denton call Moralistic Therapeutic Deism[1] – it's the label they give to the combination of beliefs that paints a benevolent but distant God who wants people to be good and fair (as taught by the main world religions) and wants his followers to find what makes them happy. Youth ministry guru Kenda Creasy Dean describes the impact of this:

The problem does not seem to be that churches are teaching young people badly, but that we are doing an exceedingly good job of teaching youth what we really believe: namely, that Christianity is not a big deal, that God requires little, and the church is a helpful social institution filled with nice people.[2]

Don't divorce them

It's impossible to divorce conversations about sex from the big story of Christianity. All too often it's in conversations with young people about sex that a misunderstanding of the invitation of the gospel is revealed. What is the gospel invitation to young people? Come to Jesus and find out who you are? Follow Jesus and find the purpose your life is craving? Become a Christian and get ready for the greatest adventure of your life?

Well, yes. In part, they're all right. We cannot fully know ourselves outside a relationship with the one who created us. God does have purposes and plans for our lives that will take us to places we never dreamed we'd go. But if we communicate that obedience to Christ is some kind of guarantee that God will help us find personal fulfilment, we're ultimately setting young people up for disappointment. Why? Because, inevitably, following Jesus means paying a cost. It's no longer about the hopes and dreams we have for our lives. Someone else is in charge.

> Calling the crowd to join his disciples, he said, 'Anyone who intends to come with me has to let me lead. You're not in the driver's seat; *I* am. Don't run from suffering; embrace it. Follow me and I'll show you how.'
> (Mark 8.34–36)

If we're not clear about the cost, young people will be receiving a nice story of self-fulfilment, but an empty gospel.

The ancient church leader, Father Tertullian, is reputed to have said, 'Just as Jesus was crucified between two thieves, so the gospel is ever crucified between these two errors.' Tim Keller calls these errors:

religion and irreligion; the theological terms are legalism and anti-nomianism. These two errors constantly seek to corrupt the message and steal away from us the power of the gospel. Legalism says that we have to live a holy, good life in order to be saved. Antinomianism says that because we are saved, we don't have to live a holy, good life.[3]

I wonder if, in our attempts to understand youth culture and to shape the gospel in a way that makes sense to their developmental stage and worldview, we've at times capitulated to antinomianism (a term coined by Reformer Martin Luther). On one level it's completely understand-able that the narrative of personal fulfilment has filtered into much of our evangelistic language with young people. We want to say to a gener-ation put off by the stereotypes (often well founded) of a church hell bent on hypocrisy and legalism that following Jesus isn't like that. And we're absolutely right to assert to young people crushed by a culture demand-ing perfection that they are loved by God *as they are* – we really don't say that loudly enough. But the pattern of discipleship presented in the Gos-pels doesn't stop there. We're loved so much that we're not left as we are.

But where the first part resonates powerfully to a generation hungry for recognition and affirmation, the second feels like a kick in the gut when you're already down, like small print that undoes the brilliance of the deal that hooked you. In that seminar, a young follower of Jesus felt the bottom fall out of what she thought she knew of God as she encountered some-thing she'd never properly considered before: that following Jesus might significantly change how she lived. My role wasn't to tell her what to do. It was to excavate that new line of thought in her. What if following Jesus meant that he would get a say on who she had sex with? That dawning re-ality can be a painful one.

More mess please, we're disciples

To put it simply, Jesus expects loving obedience from his followers. But, brilliantly, he knows we can't do this alone. We need him, we need each other, and we often need time. In our conversations with young people, we need to listen to how they're inviting Jesus into their dilemmas rather than simply feed them with the 'right' answers. This will always make for much messier discipleship.

Sometimes, sexual activity goes hand in hand with this sort of deeper discipleship stuff. Don't ignore the activity. Sometimes, young people need support accessing sexual health services, understanding consent, reporting abuse, talking with parents, etc., while at the same time needing conversations that hold space for listening to Jesus and what being faithful to him in this might be. But even as we address the activity, we must recognize that transformation is a process, a journey. It doesn't happen overnight or as the result of a one-off event or youth resource. When we say that discipleship means walking with a young person as they work this stuff out, this is the messy business we're talking about!

I remember a member of a congregation I was part of accusing me that, since my arrival at the church, there were more teenage pregnancies than before. I gently pointed out that, since I had arrived at the church, more girls who had felt totally abandoned and with no choices when they got pregnant were now finding in the church community safe spaces and adults to support them as they considered their options. As a result, more were choosing to parent rather than terminate their pregnancies. This required more from us as a church because these were young people without stability – we never knew who we might need to find emergency accommodation for. In the church, these vulnerable young people were finding a stability and a family they had not previously known. We celebrated each young life, we taught safer sex, we talked to them about consent, we called them to follow Jesus, and they were often the ones who understood life in the kingdom of God more than many of us who had grown up in the faith community.

The same is often true of young people exploring their sexuality or gender identity. A loving church that seeks to disciple young people might see more young people feeling safe to share their diverse expressions of sexual or gender identity. Rather than seeing this as a result of a lack of discipleship, it might be an indicator that we're doing a good job of creating a culture of openness that helps young people to be open to God's work in their lives.

But these conversations can make youth leaders feel uncertain, particularly if they hold 'traditional' views or belong to a church that holds to traditional teaching on marriage. 'How will the church react to this young person? How will the church react to *me*?' I've served as a youth worker in a few evangelical churches and found that, when young people felt genuinely loved within their church, they preferred to know what the church leaders thought, even if they questioned or disagreed with it. The worst thing would have been for the church leadership to have used this situation as a chance to 'harden' their theology of human sexuality and to make the young people feel that their presence or questions were causing damage to the Christian community they felt loved by.

I wonder if we're more at risk of being harmful to young people if we keep silent on our Christian sexual ethic. I know many youth leaders who are concerned that any position other than full support of a redefinition of marriage will automatically damage LGBTQ+ young people. When asked whether they agreed with what their church taught about sex, the vast majority of the Christian young people who took part in the survey said that they didn't know whether they agreed or not. This is fascinating. Could it be that young people have a greater appreciation of a diversity of views held within the church community, and don't see that as a problem in the way that older generations do? Or is it that this difference in opinion hasn't brought them into conflict with their church? It's hard to know. So we need to keep asking questions and reflecting on what we're hearing.

I've discovered that young people often want to know what the Bible teaches about sex, especially if they feel that what they think or feel may be contrary to what they read. I remember a series of conversations with a teenage boy who wanted me to help him discern what Jesus thought about him being gay. We met weekly to pray, read the Bible and watch YouTube clips of Christians who had walked the same journey. Most times we would both be in tears. Over time, he came to the conclusion that God loved him as he was and was calling him to be single and celibate. On another couple of occasions it meant helping young people find different church communities to carry on their discipleship, churches that were affirming of same-sex relationships.

To begin with, I thought it was a sign of ineffective discipleship if a young person didn't come into line with the teaching of the church, or with my reading of Scripture on a particular issue. Over time, I've come to see that God has a greater plan for young people's lives than that. As

I've stopped being afraid of what people might think of me, I've been able to tune into what God is doing in the young people's lives. I'm still learning how to have really honest conversations with young people, where I listen and speak with integrity as we explore Scripture, culture, adolescence and identity, all the while encouraging them to reach beyond me to Jesus.

Sometimes, in our desire to speak the truth to young people or to push back against a culture that doesn't hallow sex as God made it, we've not created environments at church or at home where young people are invited into the long-haul, messy wrestle of discipleship. We've wrongly assumed that, because the sexual ethics of wider culture have moved on so rapidly, young people in our churches can't cope with or aren't interested in difficult conversations about what it means to follow Jesus. If we trust that the Spirit is the greatest youth-disciple-maker the world has ever seen, we can be sure that, in the midst of all young people's wrestling with these issues, he can be trusted to gently convict, challenge and unleash young people into their full potential.

So what do we need to pay attention to in how we handle the gospel as we reimagine conversations with young people about sex?

1. Back to the basics of the gospel

The unique invitation of the gospel is to be an apprentice to Jesus of Nazareth. Built into it is the idea that you're a learner; you don't know it all. As you do the stuff Jesus did and put into practice the things Jesus taught, you will grow as a disciple and your life will look more and more like Jesus. In this paradigm, absolutely everything is affected: your approach to money, your body, your future, your time, your sexuality, your relationships, your screen life, and so on. Because of this, absolutely everything is talked about, examined and renewed in Jesus. In this paradigm, we recognize that our greatest teacher is often our mistakes. Jesus hit the road, not the small group resource, with his disciples. They discovered as they went what it meant that Jesus had 'the words of eternal life' (John 6.68, NIV). We need to expect and accept that young people will make mistakes – this should come as no surprise to us. But the gospel also speaks of a God who makes it possible for his disciples to follow him faithfully, even with all their shortcomings and struggles.

Where we stand on the gospel is of greater priority than where we stand on the particular issue of sexual identity or sexual practice, because the gospel is what invites us to become more like Jesus. The gospel includes and embraces us all. The gospel sees us all standing before the same God on judgement day. Swing too close to the conservative view and all these conversations about sex become about salvation by works. Swing too close to the liberal view and we find ineffectual grace or the 'cheap grace' that German Theologian Dietrich Bonhoeffer used to describe discipleship without cost, grace without the cross.[4] We let young people down when we make out that God is obsessed with whether we're sexually sinning or not. We let young people down when we make out that sexual sin is fine because we're already forgiven.

Conversations with young people about sex that are framed by the gospel seek to inspire them to be faithful to Jesus, whatever the cost. They are conversations that explore the topic from a cultural, personal, theological point of view, drawing in other voices and sources of wisdom. They are conversations that inspire young people to form and practise habits that help them make good decisions, drawing in the testimonies of others, and they are conversations that encourage the integration of these good habits into their character. Ultimately, they are conversations that are laced with grace and love because, if Jesus upheld a high standard of obedience and yet excessively loved those who fell short of it, we can too.[5]

2. Tell the best stories

Hearing stories of people bearing witness to the power of God in their lives is a dynamic way into conversations about sex. Testimonies are more than sharing your experience. Your experience is something that you are going through or have been through. Your testimony is what happened in that experience – what you discovered about yourself and about God. Be careful how you share or create a platform for stories of sexual sin. Some stories need to be kept private. Oversharing in an ill-advised way can lead to unintended hurt. But be careful, too, not to overemphasize the extraordinary stories to the detriment of the everyday, smaller yet powerful ones. The best stories are testimonies from Christians you know who are willing to be honest about how following Jesus is challenging and changing their attitudes, desires and practices *now*.

Another area we must pay attention to is how gender stereotypes are reinforced by the way people share their stories. I remember a teenage boy telling his friends at youth group about a sexual encounter he had with a girl at a Christian youth festival. Afterwards, he realized this had been a mistake, so he 'kicked the girl out' of his tent and said sorry to God. I was waiting for the youth leader to help the young people to see that 'kicking the girl out' wasn't what God was after. Removing or shaming her didn't absolve him. By not asking more questions of the story told, the young people were left with the headline, 'Christian boy gets rid of temptation and feels much better'. They weren't encouraged to explore why a sexual encounter outside of a covenant relationship of mutual love and commitment is not the way of Jesus. They weren't invited to think how they would approach or respond to a similar situation, or how Jesus wants them to treat others.

3. Talk about sin, shame and guilt

Sin is a problem – both because we all need saving from it and because it's a complicated concept for us to get our heads around, let alone share with young people growing up in a world of increasing faith illiteracy. Sometimes, sin is handled on a conceptual level – many of us may have inherited ideas about sin that emphasize the list of bad behaviours that make God's anger against us flare up. Because of this, we're told to make sure we avoid anything that could piss God off. Of course, it's not presented like that, but I guarantee it's heard by young people like that. In this scenario, God is a volatile dictator who needs to be appeased.

Sadly, this approach to understanding sin can lead to Christian communities seeing themselves as sin management advisors, naming the sin and shaming the sinner. If a young person has sex outside marriage or shares nudes, are these 'sins' worthy of being banned from youth cell? The resounding answer is, of course, 'no'. But the very real dilemma many of us face in teaching about sin means that sometimes we swing to the opposite, false idea of sin, that God is so accommodating of us in all our weakness that he would never put any expectations on us or steer us away from behaviours. Theologian N. T. Wright puts it brilliantly:

Some people imagine God to be always severe, always cross, always ready to find fault. Such people urgently need to discover just how kind and gracious God has been in Jesus the Messiah, and how this grace is theirs for the asking. But other people sometimes imagine that God is simply kind and generous in a sense which would rule out his ever rebuking or warning anyone about anything. Such people urgently need to discover just how much God hates evil in all its destructive and damaging ways, and how firmly he confronts, and ultimately rejects, those who persist in perpetrating it.[6]

I find it helpful to start from the position that sin is anything that separates us from that which is inherently good. Because God is good, it's a goodness defined by God's character, not ours. This is why Scripture describes sin as rebellion against God, because rebelling against God means rebelling against his good plans and purposes for the flourishing of the whole created order. Because the Bible understands sin along the lines of holiness, anything that sets itself up against God being worthy to be Lord of our lives is sin. The power of sin in the world is experienced by us as a weakness; because of the Fall, we're prone to rejecting God's plans for our flourishing because we're prone to believing lies rather than truth. Sin is a big problem, not just in individual lives, but for the entire world.

The gospel is bad news for sin and good news for us. Jesus died to save more than individuals: his mission is to make all things new. He brings a new, liberating system that will ultimately overtake and overthrow the broken systems we find ourselves in. Online porn, sex trafficking, domestic abuse, prostitution rings, transphobic bullying and gender-based violence are all things Jesus will ultimately destroy. In our conversations, we can help young people identify the power of sin at work in their world as well as in their own lives. We can start by helping them to see and lament the damage that sin causes, and the suffering, injustice, hatred, selfishness, greed and idolatry around us that we invariably also find in our own hearts. That's why we can say that, ultimately, all sin is rebellion against God. As well as needing forgiveness from those we have hurt, we must have forgiveness from God. Our conversations become these places of shelter where Paul's instruction to 'run from sexual sin' (1 Corinthians 6.18, NLT) becomes possible because what it looks like can be explored, forgiven, restored, understood, contextualized, celebrated, supported, practised and empowered.

In a desire to save young people from the damage of sexual sin, the church often fails to extend to them the space to really explore what sin is, then to admit and confess their shortcomings to God. Shame is a poor motivator, but guilt rehabilitated that leads to repentance and forgiveness can be so helpful. Young people often express a desire to put things right, to face their mistakes and find forgiveness, but they long for this within a community that doesn't hold their mistakes against them.

The church preaches about all the expectations of what we must do and gives no help or guidance so leaves us feeling lost and a failure.

[They] tell us what we can or can't do when it comes to something sexual, and it's like God changes his opinion on us based on what we have done.

4. Model what you want to see mimicked

When our children were small, Jason and I agreed that we would never say anything to them that we would need to unsay later. As both our children are adopted, it's meant being prepared to have some pretty frank chats – often way before we'd otherwise have wanted to. I remember one Christmas, when our daughter was four, she asked me in the same breath if Father Christmas was real and if she grew in my tummy. For a split second I wondered if I could fib to make her feel better. More than anything, I wanted to protect her little heart. But looking in her wide-open face, I knew I couldn't fudge the facts, not if I wanted her to trust me as a source of truth. She needed to know she would always be able to look in my eyes and know that I would speak the gentle, powerful, loving words of truth, even on the days when it would be easier not to hear the truth. Even on the days when she would struggle to believe them. I also wanted her to know that, in this family, we don't see truth as the enemy of love. We can face the tough stuff together. We can disagree and express different opinions as we all grow to be more like Jesus. We can even think differently about what the Bible means on topics and what that will mean for our lives.

In all the conversations we have with young people about sex, the witness of our lives is perhaps one of the greatest gifts we have to offer. If we're not prepared to wrestle with what it means to live out our sexuality in faithful obedience to Jesus, how will we lead others into that space of adventure and possibility? In the next chapter, we will reimagine what these engaged and resilient purity practices might look like, and how we might develop and empower them.

Outside in; inside out

Outside in

- What was the faith you inherited?
- How does your understanding of the gospel need to be stretched?
- What was your understanding of sex as a teenager? How did God feature in that?
- What shapes your understanding of how you live out your sexuality?
- How do you see a 'Disney gospel' at work in young people's thinking?
- We attribute different meanings to different sexual practices. What meaning do you give to masturbation? What meaning do you give to a young couple being physically intimate with each other? Where would you want to see Christian young people drawing boundaries around their sexual behaviour? How have you reached this conclusion? What does your church leadership think about it?
- How do the young people you know think about porn, sexting and other online sexual activities? What meaning do they give to these activities and what do you think about that?

Inside out

- What might this mean for your conversations with young people?
- How could you help young people to put Jesus at the centre of their questions and dilemmas about sex, sexuality and relationships?
- What might your youth ministry look like if you were to view conversations about sex as central to young people's discipleship?
- When we see young people's sexual development as part of their God-ordained journey into adulthood, what conversations might you want to have with a young person who is struggling with masturbation or their sexual responses and behaviours?

- Writer David Kinnaman states, 'When Millennials face turmoil, they don't just need answers from God, they need God.'[7] How could you create more space for young people to encounter Jesus in the midst of their sexual development?

6

Rebel community

That old adage, 'Don't throw the baby out with the bathwater,' always conjures up a bizarre image for me. Why would someone throw a baby out with the bathwater? Can't they feel the extra weight? Don't they realize the baby is still in the bath? OK, best not to overthink it. The clear point is that no one would do such a reckless thing – expend a huge amount of energy to throw out something that is priceless alongside something that is worthless simply because they were lumped in together.

Except, sometimes we do.

When I'm clearing out the garage or trying to declutter the house, I often get swept along in the power of the purge. Invariably, the wrong things end up in bin bags! This can happen on a global as well as on a personal level. In her book, *The Great Emergence*, author and professor of religion Phyllis Tickle spoke about how historically, every five hundred years, the Church 'cleans house'. It's a time of deciding what will and what won't be salvaged from the dominant ideas of what it means to be the Church and to follow Jesus. Tickle identified our current age as 'The Great Emergence' – the latest rummage sale in Church history. Although no one knows what this emerging Church or emerging Christianity will end up looking like, before she died in 2015, Tickle identified interesting trends that were beginning to surface. Among other things, it is radically Jesus orientated and deeply communal. Listen to online sermons, read the newest books from church leaders, download the latest podcasts and you'll hear a renewed interest in ancient practices of following Jesus – the new monasticisms and the pioneering ways of being church together in this increasingly isolated and angry age.

Earlier in the book, I sought to deconstruct aspects of the purity movement and its damaging effects on our discipleship of young people, particularly in the area of sex. The recovery period we've been

in is vital to working out what, of a biblical sexual ethic, can be rehabilitated and rediscovered in our reimagining of conversations with
young people about sex. Although we may make a mess of handling
Scripture and each other's lives when it comes to sex, we're not about
to throw the Bible under a bus. I know I'm not alone in struggling to
imagine how conversations with young people about sex that lack the
wisdom of God at their heart can ultimately bring wholeness to young
people's sexuality. In attempting *not* to throw the baby out with the
bathwater, what are we salvaging from the wreckage? What might we
need to disengage from?

This reconstruction of what the Church has to offer young people
in the way of sexual ethics is bigger than just a rejection of an evangelical purity movement. The big debates of our age all boil down to
where authority lies. Why should we teach adolescent Christians that
they shouldn't have sex before marriage? Who gets to say whether gay
marriage is acceptable or not? Who decides whether we should dissolve
all genders or not? What does a religious text written a couple of mil-
lennia ago, and bound by ancient cultural understandings of gender and
sex, have to say to emerging generations about what makes for right or
wrong sexual practices?

Youth ministry is about serving young people in Christ's name, which
means we engage Scripture as having authority over every aspect of our
work with young people. This isn't to negate the wrestling in the Church
today over what Scripture *means* when it refers to hotly contested terms
like 'one-flesh union', 'sexual immorality' and 'homosexuality', but it
is to acknowledge that, when it comes to *who* has authority to shape a
Christian sexual ethic, we start with God.

I want to make it very clear that friends of mine who hold to different
beliefs from me around masturbation, same-sex relationships, no sex
before marriage, etc., also seek to make God and Scripture their starting
point. You may be one of them. For the rest of this chapter, I share my
own understanding of discipling young people in the way of Jesus and
what that might mean for their sexual beliefs and practices. Whatever
your view of what I'm about to write, I'd like to encourage you to consider, 'What does Jesus say to young people about sex and what might
that mean for their lives?'

Jesus and sex

The world Jesus was born into was first-century Palestine. He was born into a specific time and place with cultural ideas, beliefs and practices. It was a brutal time in Israel's history, an age of radical political ideologies and violent religious nationalism. Leadership across the region was tumultuous. Herod the Great was a violent and paranoid leader (jealousy led him to kill his first wife and three of his sons). Different groups within Judaism were vying for power. The Pharisees (their name comes from the Hebrew and Aramaic *parush* or *parushi*, which means 'one who is separated') were particularly vocal in their commitment to legal traditions that were drawn less from Scripture and more from their own take on it. They saw it as their responsibility to remain aloof from any who would defile their own purity. Adherence to strict moral codes meant you could participate in the holiness of God. Around the birth of Jesus, the Levitical purity code seems to have grown in importance among a people terrified of losing their identity as God's people with the threat of being swallowed up into the superpower of Rome.

This was the backdrop to Christ's life and teaching, but the world he spoke of was radically different: the kingdom of God, the place where God reigns. This isn't a geographical location or a group of people who share a particular ethnicity or culture. The kingdom of God is the good news that God in Jesus has done what it takes to save and redeem lives, communities, even the whole world. In God's kingdom, the broken-hearted are healed, the poor are elevated, the hungry are fed, the sinners welcomed home, the powers of darkness exposed and the light of the world shines eternal. This is the reality Jesus wakes us up to and invites us to live in the truth of. God's reign provides beautiful purpose and order to our lives, including our sex lives. When Jesus and Paul talk about sex, they both point to Genesis. We're taken back to the beginning, to the place before sin drove death into our lives. And it's in this place of wholeness that we are first introduced to sex, not as a concept, but in the context of relationship: Adam and Eve's relationship.

Sex origin

The frustrating thing about the Bible is that it only really talks about what sex *is*, not what it sometimes feels like or could be. The Bible sees sex as part of God's good creation. Pre-sin. Pre-Fall. Pre-violence. Pre-greed. Sex *is* good. And sex *is* unitive – it is intended to unite two people. Scripture speaks of the one-flesh union of two sexually different individuals. It's both a physical reality (during the penetrative sex act two bodies merge as one) and it's a metaphor for God, who is other, choosing intimacy with us. The word used to describe this is a 'sacrament'. Christians throughout the ages have believed that marriage is a sacrament, a sign of a spiritual reality.

> Sex joins man and woman in intimate relationship as they become fruitful and multiply. The God who exists in utter intimacy, with love across difference at the core of his being, creates image bearers who are of the same essence but different, and calls them into one-flesh unity.[1]

Sexual intimacy within marriage is a sign of the promises of unfailing love and protection with which God binds himself to us. A Christian sexual ethic hinges on this fundamental idea of the belonging between two very 'other' beings: God and us.

Bold belonging

First, we belong to God. We're made in the image of a relational God who makes a covenant of relationship with us. In the ancient world, conquered people would sign up to a suzerain treaty with the victorious king, which would ensure their protection from other invaders and a level of autonomy in exchange for their complete allegiance to this new ruler. The stronger kingdom would adopt the weaker, conquered kingdom and its people would become citizens of this new kingdom. Allegiance to this new kingdom would result in blessings; failure to live up to their side of the agreement would result in the curse of being abandoned. Nice. A widely used rite was that of dead animals being cut in half and laid on the ground with enough space for the two making the agreement to walk between the pieces. By doing so, they were vowing, 'May what has happened to these animals, happen to me if I break this covenant with you.'[2] This is in essence the treaty that God invites

Abraham into in Genesis 15.9–21. But contrary to the covenant usually made between a victor and the vanquished in the ancient world, in this instance God alone passes through the pieces of the dead animal. God alone seals the covenant – it's not dependent on Abraham. God is saying that, if either side breaks the promise of allegiance, God will suffer. Which he does.

The salvation that we find in Christ is a continuation of this covenant promise that flows throughout the biblical narrative. Our belonging to God comes at a price – our allegiance to him as our rescuing king. One of the most popular pictures in the New Testament to describe salvation is adoption. We belong to God because we've been adopted into God's family – it's the highest calling on our lives. Adopting us cost God dearly; Scripture speaks of us being 'bought at a price' (1 Corinthians 6.20, NIV). It's a belonging forged in God's blood in the death of Christ. What God has done can never be undone. We're never unadopted from God's family, never kicked out or cancelled.

But as well as understanding ourselves as adopted into God's family, we're called into union with God. It's a love that nothing can separate us from. If shame is in essence a fear of unbelonging, the truth that we belong to God because of an act of God is the greatest antidote to fear and shame. Our bodies are places both where we experience this unfailing love of God and through which we give shape to what it looks like to belong to God. Our bodies point to the truth that we belong to God. Our relationship to God is not expressed only in the ideas we have about God, or even in the feelings about God. Our belonging to God is evident in how our allegiance to our rescuing king is demonstrated through how we value and use our bodies.

'Do you not know that your bodies are temples of the Holy Spirit?' Paul asks the new Christians in Corinth (1 Corinthians 6.19, NIV). 'You're a temple of worship,' Paul is saying. 'You're a place where God's holy presence is, so treat your body as belonging to him, *not to you*.' This isn't to denigrate and dismiss our bodies. Our bodies are precious to God. Our physicality, sexuality, sensuality are all part of this glorious belonging to God and are places where our allegiance is declared. We don't need to cease to be an embodied person to belong fully to God. The truth that our bodies are the place where God dwells with us gives breathtaking purpose and shape to our sexuality. In fact, the Bible doesn't shy away from saying that the kind of intimate union that's experienced between lovers points the way to the deeper union that we have with God (see, for example, Isaiah 62.5b; Jeremiah 31.3; Zephaniah 3.17).

This brings us to the second belonging that shapes a Christian sexual ethic: marriage. This is the practice Jesus celebrates and elevates when he quotes to the Pharisees, 'For this reason a man will leave his father and mother and be united to his wife, and the two will become one flesh' (the Hebrew is *basar echad*) (Matthew 19.5, NIV, citing Genesis 2.24). The few times Jesus talks about God's design for sex, he speaks about the one-flesh union between sexually different individuals. The question is whether anything else can be included in this one-flesh idea. Does Jesus' teaching on sex allow for same-sex sexual relationships or prohibit them among his followers? These are questions we need to wrestle with.

It's worth noting that Jesus isn't just fixating on the moment of penetrative sex for this 'one-flesh' switch to be flipped. He's referring to the whole story of Adam and Eve's creation: Adam being alone; God forming Eve out of Adam's body; God presenting Eve to Adam; Adam recognizing her as not only from his body but also from God; their shared commitment to rule over the earth and populate it *and*, last but not least, their physical intimacy. The stream of biblical teaching that Jesus is endorsing is one that views sex as a life-uniting reality between two sexually different individuals that points us to the unbreakable bond God has formed with us.

These two tracks of belonging (bodily union with God and sexual union between two sexually different individuals) underpin my view of a Christian sexual ethic: faithfulness to God and faithfulness to each other. Love of God *is* faithfulness to God. Love of your spouse *is* faithfulness to your spouse. Imagine a relationship where one person says to the other, 'I love you but I just don't want to be faithful to you.' That person's unfaithfulness would put a question over the sincerity of his or her love, because faithfulness *is* love.

Over the years, I've walked with many young Christians as they've explored what it means to be faithful to God in how they embrace and express their sexuality. When they ask me what I think the Bible means, I tell them the conclusion I'm coming to through a lot of listening – to

God, to others, to the Bible. I also tell them that there are Christians who are also praying, listening well and studying Scripture and coming to different conclusions. I explain that I want to be open with them about what I believe, because it's a way of me being faithful to them, but my faithfulness to them doesn't stop with me just sharing my view. My faithfulness to them continues in how I extend grace and love as they work it out. If they've got questions about sexuality, they're welcome in the youth group and the church family. If they go 'too far' with someone or do something they regret, they're welcome in the youth group and the church family. If they 'come out' as gay, they're welcome in the youth group and the church family. If they bring their non-Christian, gay, queer or questioning partner to church, they're both welcome in the youth group and the church family. We extend to all young people the same opportunities for getting involved in leadership, with boundaries and expectations for growing in godly character and servant heartedness. The young people who step into positions of spiritual leadership in my church context know this means that (within the loving environment of support and grace) we expect them to be committed to sexual restraint in terms of no sexual intimacy with anyone outside marriage, to set strong boundaries around their porn, sex-tech and social media use, and to model Jesus-style love and selflessness in all their interactions with others.

Finding faithfulness

At the beginning of this chapter, I asked you to consider what you think Jesus is asking from his followers when it comes to how they order their sex lives. What does *your* response to this mean in terms of how you have conversations with young Christians about sex? How will your conversations be framed by your desire to see them grow as disciples of Jesus?

I want to suggest that, however you answer that, you and I probably make the same mistake – we put the focus on what it means for *us* to be faithful to God: what decisions and practices make us more or less faithful, more or less holy? But the emphasis in Scripture is always on *God's* faithfulness. Time and again, our ancestors in the faith demonstrate that even when we are faithless, God is faithful. A Christian sexual ethic doesn't start with teaching no sex before marriage or that as long as it's faithful and consensual, sexual intimacy can honour God. It starts with encountering the faithfulness of God. This is liberating. If God is no less faithful to a young person who has sex outside marriage than to a young person who remains chaste, we can be confident in the knowledge that, as young people make mistakes, nothing will change God's faithfulness to them.

It needs repeating that young people who are following Jesus *will make mistakes when it comes to sex*. Older Christians make mistakes when it comes to sex. God is under no illusions about this, even though we often behave as if he is expecting perfection from us. God alone is faithful all the time; the rest of us struggle. And yet it's often in this struggle that we experience God's faithfulness in greater measure. If this is true, let's be bolder in walking young people into the repentance and restoration that is always available for them.

Of course, young people in our church youth group might not want to be faithful to God. If that's the case, I'm not expecting them to want to express that in sexual practices that honour him. I think that's worth repeating: if someone isn't a follower of Jesus, I don't expect them to be obedient to him in anything, let alone their sex lives. I'll support them to make healthy choices around their safety and well-being, but I won't expect them to want God to be a part of this.

Another likelihood is that young people in our church communities might want to belong to God without wanting to live a holy life. Forcing young people to adopt a set of practices because we or they think it's the 'right' thing to do when they're not convinced isn't discipleship. If the young people we serve aren't ready yet or interested in exploring what it means to live a holy life, our focus needs to be on helping them be open to the wonder and wildness of who God is and what it means to belong to him. Conversations about sex probably won't need to take centre stage. But when they do, let's be ready.

But there might be young people who are ready to step into what following Jesus means. They will need to take small, steady, supported and celebrated steps along this path. Just like I do now. Just as you do. Step by step, walking in the way of Jesus. Repenting of mistakes. Deepening in love of God. Growing in Christlikeness.

Holiness is not about you

So many of us have grown up in churches where sex became the easiest way to explain holiness: you stay holy if you avoid sexual practices outside marriage. With enough social shame generated to make it stick, this teaching inevitably formed a toxic connection in our brains between shame and sex, between our bodies and our belonging to God. When God and sex are pitted against each other, sex invariably wins out, either because we end up having sex before marriage (secretive, sometimes great and nearly always guilt-ridden sex) or because we become obsessed with not having it (leading us to see our sexual desires as evil and our bodies as dangerous). We wrongly believe it is within our power to make ourselves holy. To clean up the mess. To make sure other people stick to the strict rules too. To see them as a problem when they don't.

This reduction of holiness to a list of certain sexual behaviours causes serious problems for our sexuality and discipleship. If we can so quickly lose our holiness by a physical act, the focus of our discipleship has to be on avoiding at all costs any behaviour that would risk me losing my connection to God. But the offence of holiness is that we don't get to say what makes us or anyone holy. In essence, holiness isn't about us. Holiness is about God and about who God declares to be holy.

Paul casts a different vision of holiness: we're dead people who have come to life, and this resurrection life is growing, unfurling in us (see Ephesians 2.1, Romans 6.3–4). It's sanctification not hinged on restrictive codes that keep us on the safe side of sin, but on staying close to the Father. It's in this close belonging with the Father that we begin to recognize that, left to our own devices, we often choose to order our sex lives in ways that don't honour God, ourselves or others. It's in this close proximity of belonging to the Father that this knowledge doesn't destroy us, but instead allows us to surrender and receive forgiveness, mercy and strength to live differently.

This is where the wonder of holiness reaches another level for me. Rather than a standard to achieve, it is an identity I receive as this new life takes shape in me. I *am* holy. I *am* set apart. I *am* pure. I *am* God's. And my focus now is to live as someone liberated *by* and *for* God. This is the only hope I have to know a life free from endless self-definition, obsessive sin-monitoring, controlling self-delusion, addictive and damaging habits and loading hurt and shame on myself and others. Because of Jesus, this new creation life is possible. And what's more, even when I'm struggling, I am *still* a new creation, I am *still* holy, and this is all part of the unfurling into the person God made me to be.

If holiness isn't something we *do*, but something we *are* because of our new creation in Christ, why does Paul talk in 2 Corinthians 7.1 about 'perfecting holiness out of reverence for God' (NIV)? If we're holy because we're set apart for God, how can we become any more or less holy? In the verses before, Paul tells us that, as we respond to God's invitation to 'be holy, because I am holy' (1 Peter 1.16, NIV), God promises to receive us as his adopted children. As an adoptive parent, this intrigues me. When did our children become ours? My husband and I heard their names from our social worker, read their profiles, painted their bedrooms, laid our lives out to be scrutinized, signed the paperwork, brought them home, attended court hearings, received the legal documentation, sat up with them at night when they couldn't sleep, cheered when they called us 'Mum' and 'Dad', cried when they said, 'I love you.' In all of this, when did they belong to us? The answer is at every stage, but also in deepening ways every day.

God takes the initiative to draw us to himself. He alone cleans our lives from anything that would separate us from him (see 1 John 1.9). But when Paul speaks of 'perfecting holiness', he's not talking about getting the top mark to earn holiness. He uses a word that speaks of completeness, wholeness. It's the idea that, as well as being made holy by God, we get to walk towards the wholeness we discover in the freedom of belonging to God. Some biblical scholars call this 'progressive sanctification', meaning that we become more like Jesus as we're transformed by the Spirit *over time*. This ongoing transformation inevitably creates tension in us with how we used to live and with the way things are around us in culture. Paul got that: 'the old me is dead,' he wrote, 'and the new me is working this stuff out in fear and trembling' (see Philippians 2.12; Galatians 2.20).

Over time not overnight

If I think of the older teenagers in my church community, I see in them a wild desire to be radical in their faith without having to repress or disengage from their sexual selves. I'm encouraged by this, even if I feel constantly that I'm in new territory with them. These past few years, I've noticed an increase in conversations with Christian young people longing for their church to help them establish sexual boundaries, but without heavy guilt and shame if they transgress those boundaries.

In the survey, I asked what is the worst thing a church could do for Christian young people when it comes to conversations about sex. The replies came thick and fast. All on the same general theme – 'Don't judge us when we get this wrong.'

> We want to know that if we have gotten involved in anything that we are still loved just as much as before and we are forgiven. We don't want to feel shame in asking questions or sharing certain experiences.

> I want someone to tell me that God won't punish me for messing up, something I can't come to terms with as I believe God will punish me for doing anything so I'm avoiding doing too much out of fear.

There were hundreds of comments like these. This is the heart cry from a generation of young disciples caught between a church that teaches sexual restraint and a culture that believes if we express sexual restraint, or don't act on sexual urges, we are being dualistic in our thinking (body is bad, spirit is good). When this is twinned with an extreme within public discourse that demands we should always be protected from discomfort and offence, young people are left completely unsure how to set boundaries around sex and how to handle any guilt they may feel around making mistakes. Against these backdrops, how do we support young followers of Jesus to be radically, defiantly faithful to God in the whole of their lives, including their sex lives, in a way that is both grounded in practical support and infused with vision and promise? How do we do this in a way that doesn't overshadow their lives and intimate relationships with guilt, shame, disgust and sexual repression? In the words of another ancient youth-disciple-maker, how can we ensure our conversations with young people about sex are 'always full of grace, seasoned with salt, so that you may know how to answer everyone' (Colossians 4.6, NIV). The second part of this book looks in more detail into how we can do this.

Outside in; inside out

Instead of responding to a series of questions, take a moment to pause. Breathe. Make this a moment between you and the God who created and loves you. Everything he calls you to do flows from the truth that you belong to him.

Imagine you hold in your hands everything you have to offer a young person on their journey of sexual and faith maturity. Some of it may be wisdom drawn from your own painful experiences. Some of it may be strengths you've had since birth or skills honed over a lifetime. Some of it may be what you're daily discovering of God's grace, restoration and strength. But even with all you have to bring (and it's more than you think), it's impossible to predict what a move of the Spirit in young people's lives will look like as you hold space for them to be safe, to be challenged and to be equipped. You can enter each conversation alert to the signs of how God is already at work in the young person's life, so that you can respond with the maximum amount of compassion, wisdom and creativity the moment allows.

Whether our resources are plentiful or scarce, may we commit to serving young people well as we walk them towards a life of rebel, joyful holiness.

May they meet God in us, and may we meet God in them, and may it transform us both.

Part 2

The most important thing that a church can do to support Christian young people in the area of sex is to stop treating sex like it's the biggest sin. If we can have conversations about sex like we do for lying, without judgement, then we would be more honest and open about it and, ultimately, we would all feel less lonely.
Young person, A Christian Youth Sex Survey

The life-giving Spirit of GOD will hover over him,
the Spirit that brings wisdom and understanding,
The Spirit that gives direction and builds strength,
the Spirit that instills knowledge and Fear-of-GOD.
Fear-of-GOD will be all his joy and delight.
He won't judge by appearances,
won't decide on the basis of hearsay . . .
Each morning he'll pull on sturdy work clothes and boots,
and build righteousness and faithfulness in the land.
Isaiah 11.2–3, 5

Please talk! I think not communicating anything at all is worse than saying something that some people might not agree with. It makes 'sex' seem such a dirty, secretive thing.
Young person, A Christian Youth Sex Survey

7

Let's talk about sex

Some of the best conversations about sex aren't really about sex at all – or at least, they don't start out that way. We often stumble into important topics with young people as we're packing away at the end of a youth session or over a hot chocolate while sitting with teenagers on a kerb. Conversations don't need to be long to be significant. At other times, what starts off as a chat about prayer turns into a discussion about whether oral sex *is* sex or whether Jesus thinks it's acceptable for one of his followers to have a relationship with someone who isn't one of his followers. This is what makes working among young people so interesting and so humbling – you never really know what conversations you might find yourself in. But this doesn't mean that we don't need to prepare or have some understanding of how we can host good conversations with young people about sex.

Good conversations with a safe and wise adult, whether pre-planned or spontaneous, are essential to a young person's well-being. This is true of every topic, and it's especially true of sex. Research shows time and again that providing accurate, timely information doesn't increase sexual activity. In fact, it leads to fewer risk-taking behaviours.[1] Being listened to increases young people's self-esteem, helping them to recognize their own value and raise their aspirations to make healthy, informed choices for themselves. Talking with trusted adults helps young people develop a language and framework to process what they're going through. For young people growing up in a Christian faith environment this is especially important, as the story of sex told in church is often at odds with the rapidly shifting sexual ethics in wider culture. By creating the context for healthy conversations around sexuality, we're providing a good context for young people to succeed and flourish in their teenage years and beyond.

At the heart of our conversations needs to be young people's sexual well-being as God intends it. The goal isn't to stop a teenager from having sex or to keep a church leader or Christian parent happy. The goal is to enable a young person to develop their own thinking and practices in the light of what it means to follow Jesus. Even if part of this process is them questioning or even rejecting faith, our role is to equip them to make decisions that are well informed, free from coercion and a result of a good examination of all the issues.

Full of well-being

Sexual well-being is more than being free from harm (although this is part of it). It's experiencing a fullness of well-being that covers every aspect of sexuality and sexual health. When Jesus promises to give his followers peace (John 14.27; 20.19, 21, 26), he uses the Hebrew word *shalom*, which describes the life in all its fullness that God creates (see John 10.10). 'The root meaning of the word *shalom* is wholeness, completeness and well-being. It includes health, security, friendship, prosperity, justice, righteousness and salvation, all of which are necessary if wholeness, completeness and well-being are to come about.'[2]

At its heart, *shalom* is reconciliation to God. It is a reconciliation that leads to the kind of wholeness and well-being that only God can give. Paul directly links the shedding of Christ's blood on the cross with the reality of *shalom* in the lives of Christ's followers (Colossians 1.19–20). On the cross, Jesus 'experiences infinite pain so that we can know endless peace'.[3] It is because Jesus reconciles us to God that we can live under God's sovereignty, experiencing life as God always intended for us. This inward sense of completeness transforms our interactions and relationships with others.

In places where *shalom* is used as a greeting, it denotes a desire for the other person to be full of well-being. Paul's regular prayer for the early church was that they would be full of well-being: 'Now, may the Lord himself, the Lord of peace, pour into you his peace in every circumstance and in every possible way. The Lord's *tangible* presence be with you all' (2 Thessalonians 3.16, TPT).

Young people's sexual well-being as God intends encompasses their safety, health, relationships, desires and integrity as followers of Jesus.

One doesn't need to take priority because, when they're all embraced as areas for good, godly conversation, young people are free to explore and experience the sexual well-being that obedience to Jesus enables them to know. Over years of listening to young people's questions and concerns about sex, I've noticed that, on the whole, they boil down to five areas included in a scriptural understanding of *shalom*. The five topics are (in the order they appear in the book, but *not* in order of priority):

- The sexual health thing: conversations to do with accurate information about bodies, sexual activity (with reproductive and non-reproductive aims), the menstrual cycle, puberty, sexual health, STIs (sexually transmitted infections) and pregnancy, as well as sexual health services and support.
- The safety thing: conversations about safer sex and freedom from sexual behaviour that is unwanted or makes young people feel uncomfortable or afraid. This includes freedom from being spoken to in a sexualized way or with sexualized language, as well as freedom from seeing someone acting in a sexual way towards them or others they are with, including nakedness, masturbation, exposure or being shown pornographic images.
- The desire thing: conversations about sexual responses and arousal, as well as young people's choices around sexual attraction and activity. It's an exploration of how their desires can lead them to be courageous in opening themselves up to God and others.
- The intimacy thing: conversations to do with trust and vulnerability in friendships as well as sexual relationships. It's about young people growing in appreciation of how to build intimate connections with others, understanding the impact of closeness.
- The integrity thing: conversations to do with young people exercising their sexual agency and power with honesty and wisdom. It's about them growing in the strength of moral character to make choices that are consistent with what they believe to be the purpose of sex, even when others aren't looking or don't share their beliefs or values.

The young people's context will shape what they bring to the conversation. The purpose behind splitting 'sex' into five topic areas is to help you ensure that, in your own thinking and discipleship of young people, you're not prioritizing one issue at the expense of another. You will find there is huge overlap between these five areas so please don't feel restricted to only talking about one aspect with young people – I'm not imagining that you will have five separate conversations, one for each topic. Instead, the idea is that you pay attention to what the young people are talking about and what other things they might need to know or explore. Whether your conversations are planned or spontaneous, the material under each of these topics will equip you to support and guide the young people.

How to have a conversation about sex

Not all young people seek out conversations for the same reasons. Some may be wanting to process an experience. Others may have seen something online or have come across an idea or question they want clarity on. Still others may be experiencing changes in their bodies that feel unsettling, or they may be facing a relationship dilemma and need reassurance and guidance on how to approach it. I find that conversations about sex can often start with young people expressing concern about a friend or wanting to talk about something they're heard. One thing is certain – young people will only know that they can have these conversations with you *if you let them know they can*. As well as being ready for a young person who asks to chat, how can you be making it clear that young people in your church, youth group or family setting can reach out to you for a conversation about sex? And once they do, how will you host that conversation?

Let me introduce you to ALEGRA.[4] ALEGRA is an acronym to give you a helpful framework for any conversation with young people about sex. Ensure you follow your church or organization's safeguarding practices and policies when seeking to utilize this framework or engaging young people in any conversation.

A is for ASK

How will you make yourself available to a young person so that they know they can ask you for a chat? Think about who you could engage in conversations with and how you will ensure conversations are safe. Don't assume that only 'certain' young people in your church might want to talk about sex. Those who look like they have 'got it all together' might be crying out for someone to talk to. Be intentional about how each young person might need to hear the invitation to have chats with a trusted adult about anything to do with sex. Focus on being approachable so that if the young people want to talk with you, they feel more confident to do so.

Begin each conversation by asking the young person what they want to ask or talk about.

L is for LISTEN

Listen to what the young people are saying. Avoid finishing their sentences for them and ensure your body language and reactions are supportive and non-judgemental. You're creating an undefended space where no one is arguing their case or trying to change someone's mind. Instead, you're listening with love and with a desire to learn and understand (not to make your point). If they have presented a question or a dilemma, you may feel tempted to jump in with your solution. Resist this.

E is for EXPLORE

It is well documented that, to ensure they are able to make healthy and confident choices, young people need:

- accurate information and relevant knowledge;
- personal judgement, often referred to as self-efficacy, which is the sense of what negative consequences could mean for them and others and their perceived control over their decisions;
- space to practise and perfect the skills they need (like decision-making, communication and refusal skills);
- support from a community to help them maintain healthy behaviours.

I've combined these into three areas of conversation that I've called 'Exploring the What', 'Exploring the How' and 'Exploring the Why'. Leading young people through these equips them with what they need to deal with different situations, know their own mind and feel confident to form and maintain healthy sexual practices. You may find they need a combination of all these sorts of questions, but it's more likely that you will want to focus on one of the exploring aspects. If this is the first conversation you're having on this topic or it's with a pre-teen or very young teenager, you'll probably want to focus on the What section. If the young person is needing support to know what to do or how to respond, focus on the How section. For older young people who are seeking to put their faith identity at the centre of their vision for their sexuality and sex lives, focus on the Why section. But go with your instinct as you listen.

1. Exploring the What

Considering what young people want and need to know about sex
Your focus is on helping young people access accurate information and relevant knowledge on the issue they've raised. You might start with helping the young people identify what they're currently facing or thinking, and what they might want to talk with you about. As you listen, it might be clear that you need to correct misinformation or help them access or identify good information or knowledge. You might want to spark interest or curiosity in other ways of seeing this topic – what the Bible, their church tradition and the Holy Spirit might be saying to them about it – and what they think about that. Use open questions – for example,

- What's making you most curious about this topic, and why?
- What sorts of things do you hear people at school or online talk about?
- What do you want to know more about?
- What annoys you most about this topic?
- What do you think about . . .?

2. Exploring the How

Helping young people explore what they are going to do
Your focus is on helping the young people to develop some skills and healthy habits about the issue they've raised. This equips them to explore their sexual development without needing to be sexually active. Rather than simply asking what they think or feel about something, you're helping them consider *how* they might behave based on their beliefs or ideas, and how they might feel about and deal with the consequences. Use open questions, for example:

- How do you feel about the decision you're making?
- How do you feel about enacting it?
- How are you working out which consequences are OK and which will deter you?
- How will you put your decision into action?
- How are you handling mistakes or dealing with consequences you didn't predict?
- How are you growing in your relationship with God/your Christian faith identity?

3. Exploring the Why

Supporting young people to dig deeper into how this aspect of sex fits into the bigger picture of living with God at the centre of their lives

Your focus is on the young people's understanding of why they believe what they believe. Depending on age and stage, use questions that reframe what they're wrestling with in terms of their understanding of who God is and how God acts in the world. The goal is to help the young people to see their decisions in the light of their commitment to follow Jesus. Use open questions, such as:

- What do you believe God is saying to you about this, and how are you responding to that?
- What are you wrestling/struggling with?
- What is that telling you about your deeper desires?
- How is this bringing you closer to God, or encouraging you to seek after God more?
- What are you finding it difficult to let go of?
- What are you finding it difficult to talk to God about?

G is for GIVE

Once you've finished exploring with the young people their thoughts and ideas about the topic, think about what input you could bring. Think of your contribution as a gift, not a sermon. Is there a passage in Scripture or some clarity you could bring around a belief or practice? Is there anything from your own life experience that could help the young people see from a different perspective what they're going through?

If you have some input to bring, here are some pointers to help you to do that well. First, rather than simply saying, 'This is what the Bible says about . . .', you could read the passage together and ask, 'Why do you think God says/the Bible says this?' Make it clear that you're not looking for a set answer; instead, you're interested in helping them grow in curiosity and willingness to hear from God. Encourage waiting on the Holy Spirit as you read a passage or consider a story together. Demonstrate that it's possible to change your mind about something. This side of eternity we don't know everything, only God does, and it's good to hold our convictions and our questions with humility.

Second, encourage the young people to widen their circle of friends and listen to a wider range of voices. Is there a book or podcast you could listen to and discuss together? Share how you discern what voices you will listen to and why. Are there some that you listen to but don't give a lot of influence to in your life? Are there voices that you are willing to allow to challenge you to the core, if need be? One good question to ask is, 'Name one person who you think knows more about this than you and is living a life that honours Jesus. What can you learn from them?'

R is for REFLECT

Reflection gives the young people pause to problem-solve for themselves. It's deeply empowering as it puts the power to make their decisions into their hands. This can feel daunting, even anxiety inducing, for young people who haven't been encouraged to think for themselves. So don't be afraid to hold silence and keep reassuring them as they share their thoughts. Use phrases like, 'I would love to hear what's stood out for you from this conversation,' and, 'I wonder what you might do differently as a result of this conversation.'

A is for ASK AGAIN

As you finish, you could enquire how the young people have found the conversation with you and whether they would like to meet again to keep the conversation going. You might like to ask whether they want to broaden the conversation to include other things that might be relevant (you could suggest other topics taken from the headings on p. 109). If they don't seem keen to meet with you again, don't take it personally (easier said than done!). But we want the young people to know they can access conversations with trusted adults, even if that's not with us! Ask them how they might want you to help them find someone. Ask for feedback from them about how you could do chats like these better!

Sometimes, we leave prayer until the end of a conversation or session as a way to wrap things up. Consider praying at different times during your conversation – brief, to-the-point prayers that demonstrate that God is at the centre of this conversation and is compassionately invested in their lives.

All inclusive[5]

There can be a myth within churches and wider society that young people with additional needs don't do sex. It comes from the mistaken notion of the never-ending child who doesn't grow up so never experiences adult things, including sex. This misconception can leave young people with additional needs unprepared for the changes that are happening to their bodies and feelings and increases their vulnerability to exploitation and sexual harm. If young people's additional needs mean it's hard for them to comprehend and express what's happening (in terms of puberty as well as abuse or exploitation), it can be difficult for them to access the information and support they need to be safe. As precious and valued members of our church and youth group with a huge amount to contribute, it's important that young people with additional needs have opportunities to access safe, supportive and positive conversations with us about sex. As each young person with additional needs is unique, just like all young people, it's important that we take the time to listen to where they are coming from and to learn from them how we can best create space where they feel safe, understood and really appreciated.

In a lot of cases (although not all), parents or carers of young people with additional needs will know what support they are receiving in other settings, such as school, and will be able to point you to resources that you could draw on, replicate or adapt to use in your conversations with them (one-page profiles are an excellent way to find out more about young people and how best to support them). This continuity between school life, home life and church/youth group life can help the young people feel confident and safe to grow. Think about making contact with their teacher or support worker so you can learn about methods of communication that they are familiar with and what concepts around sex, relationships or life skills they're learning about at school.

Some of the best sex education training I've received was when I supported staff and sexual health nurses at an additional needs school, working with young people to build their understanding and skills around sexual consent. What training could you access to equip you in conversations about sex with a young person in your youth group who has additional needs?[6] Think about how you could develop a stronger link with the family of the young person so that the church can offer wider support to the whole family. There are a range of organizations and resources for you to tap into. Social stories[7] are a well-used resource for young people with additional needs that take a new, complex or different learning concept and makes it easier for them to understand, using symbols or pictures to support text. Each social story takes a young person on a journey through an aspect of puberty, sex or relationships, building layers of communication and understanding that are tailored to his or her specific ways of learning.

Using these and other tools, such as one-page profiles, helps young people feel better prepared for all they are facing in their bodies, emotions and social environments.

The five sex things

Each of the following chapters will focus on a different element of sex. The aim is to equip *you* for whatever conversation you find yourself in or invite a young person into. These are not intended for use as session plans or even as guides to what to say. Instead, they focus on how *your* theological reflections, personal convictions and experiences, knowledge of the topics, compassion for the young people, commitment to their flourishing and openness to the Holy Spirit can be brought into each conversation.

Scripture has much to say about the power of wise counsel in the life of young people and the awe-inspiring responsibility placed on our shoulders as we are called to walk faithfully with them. We may feel daunted, even anxious, as we step into these conversations. That's OK. Being aware of the importance of these moments with young people can ensure we approach them with humility. Let's do all we can to listen well, speak with grace and truth, and remain committed to being voices that aid their sexual well-being. Go for it!

8

The sexual health thing

A while ago, I sat with a group of teenagers (aged between eleven and thirteen) and asked them to write down all the words they've ever heard of that relate to sexual reproduction. 'Like babies?' one girl asked. 'Yeah, babies, sex, periods, erections . . .' I replied. 'Any words or phrases you've heard people use that have something to do with having sex, having babies. Anything.'

Once they realized they wouldn't get into trouble for using 'bad words', they threw themselves into writing down all the words they've heard people use to describe sex (bang, poke, smash, hit, 53X), body parts (schlong, shrimpy, pussy, anaconda, slash, hole, pole), having sex (kill it, Netflix and chill, bonk, doing the nasty, getting some, hooking up, getting down and dirty, NIFOC 'Naked in front of computer'), not having sex (frigid), being rejected romantically (curve, ghosting), being badly treated in a relationship (gaslighting), or to describe girls after they've had sex (walk of shame, nasty) or boys after they've had sex (man points, boi, dog).

'What do you think of all these words?' I asked.

'Harsh!' one boy replied.

'It's really unequal!' a girl interjected. 'Boys are like, "Look at me, I've had sex!" and girls get called a slut for having sex.'

'What words could people use to talk about sex that would make it more equal or less harsh?' I asked.

'Don't know. It's not like we're going to say, "Oh, shall we have sexual intercourse?"' one boy replied, 'or "make love"!'

Everyone sniggered, almost as if they were more embarrassed by this than any of the terms they'd previously been writing down.

'What don't you like about the phrase, "making love"?' I asked.

'Who says that any more? No one says that!' another girl piped up.

Language matters

She's right.

Words matter. Using the correct terminology, or just not using derogatory language, doesn't win a young person social rewards in a culture that has a very coded way of talking about sex. Sexual banter, underhand comments, double entendre, slang and veiled meanings all create a complicated web of communication. How young people talk in their peer groups about sex is a brilliant example of how conversations can be both revealing and concealing at the same time – they may sound like they all know what's being talked about when that isn't always the case. Some young people think it's safer to simply snigger at others rather than risk getting it 'wrong'. Assuming that young people know more about sex than you do because of 'the world they're growing up in', or because of their behaviours or friends, might result in them not receiving factually and medically accurate information about sex from a trusted source. This could put them more at risk.

Sometimes, adults who are not yet sexually active think they are not the 'best person' to talk with young people who might already be experimenting sexually. Nothing could be further from the truth. You don't need to be an expert or even find it easy to talk about sex to be a good person for young people to talk with. Conversations with young people about sex are not about sharing *your* sexual experiences. They are about helping them access and understand accurate information in a timely way, and to know how to use the information.

As sex education is an ongoing conversation, often the best way to start is by dealing with facts and information about puberty, bodies and sexual reproduction. Of course, facts and figures can make anything dry and boring, but for many pre-teens and young teens who are finding their feet in conversations about such a huge a topic as sex, this approach can be really effective. It gives them a positive outlet for their natural curiosity and helps them to develop appropriate language and supportive relationships with trusted adults who will walk with them on their journey of sexual maturation.

It's good to consider *how* you talk about sex and bodies. Think about being clear and credible in your use of language – try not to use the word 'it' when you could be more specific about what you're referring to. Avoid using words that don't sit well with you. If a young person says 'dick' and you would be more comfortable with 'penis', then use the word 'penis'. You can do this without shaming a young person. They're not wrong to use words they feel comfortable with or have grown up using, but by you using a wider range of accurate terms, you're helping them to explore ways to talk about sex with more clarity and maturity.

Another area to consider is your tone and body language. As a teenager, I always knew when my mum was gearing up for a serious conversation with me because she would use 'the voice' that was reserved for reading the Bible or praying out loud at church. Sex is a serious matter with serious consequences, but we don't need to ignore the molehill, nor make a mountain out of it. We can talk constructively about sex without sounding like the nightly newsreader. A warm, kind tone will serve young people far better than being stern and serious. It's all right to laugh with a young person about something you both find funny. On the other hand, it's important that we're not adding to the sexual banter that dominates the way sex is talked about in culture. Often this is subtle and may even seem playful, but as adults in positions of power in young people's lives, we are not creating a safe space for them if we are speaking to them in ways that ridicule them, or if we make them feel uncomfortable with a joke about sex. The Apostle Paul gives a stunning argument for watching the way we talk: 'Say only what helps,' he implores, 'each word a gift' (Ephesians 4.29).

So let's look at how we can help young people explore the what, how and why questions around sexual reproduction.

Exploring the What

Considering what young people want and need to know about sexual health
The best way to find out what young people want to know is to ask them. It sounds obvious, but it's a good way to gauge where the young people are in their knowledge of a topic. They may just shrug, in which case you can suggest things they might like to know more about. But it's also worth considering how you will share relevant information in a way that not only informs them of the facts but also helps them connect their faith with their sexual development.

You'd be amazed at how many myths around sex young people believe. Myths take many forms, from, 'You can't get pregnant if you have sex standing up,' to, 'Sex is shameful, so God wants you to save it for the person you love.' Many young people growing up in church would say that God created sex – and they'd be right. But when pressed, this is often more about morality (what you can or can't do) than anything else.

Before conversations about boundaries around behaviours, it's helpful for young people to understand why God chose sexual reproduction as the way for ensuring the survival of a species. God didn't need to and, as far as Darwinism is concerned, sexual reproduction doesn't make a lot of sense. Asexual reproduction, where an individual organism can replicate itself entirely, is a far more effective method of keeping the species going in terms of both success rate and purity of the genetic material (although from an evolutionary perspective this genetic purity can also be seen as stagnation). In that single-sex scenario, no one is having to waste time finding a mate who is fertile. No one is concerned about the new mix of genes when half the male and half the female chromosomes are united in the zygote. No one is worried that the reproductive rate of the species is seriously reduced when only half of the population can produce offspring. And yet, when it comes to humans (and most animals), God designed reproduction where a male and a female contribute something of themselves into each new life created. They give from their own lives to make this new life.

Sexual reproduction, as the process of keeping the species going, requires a male and a female who have reached physical sexual maturity to unite in the act of a penis entering a vaginal passage to create offspring. The offspring need a whole load of care and protection as they grow and develop into sexually mature beings who can, in turn, meet, mate, give birth to, protect and raise the next generation. Thanks to modern medicine, we can give assistance to people who struggle to conceive in this way. This is sometimes called IVF (in vitro fertilization), but there is a wide range of ways that science can assist the process of reproduction. Human biology is both beautiful and mysterious.

This doesn't mean that every time a heterosexual couple have vaginal sex they will (or should) conceive a baby, or that the *only* purpose for sexual intimacy is reproduction, but it gives great dignity to human bodies as co-creators, with God, of life itself.

Where this intersects with young people is that it provides a wider framework for seeing that their sexual development is good. Their bodies, including their sex organs and secondary sexual characteristics, are good. Their curiosities and questions about what's happening to them during puberty are good. This goodness of sex and of their bodies is an essential message to communicate because it is the bedrock for healthy sexual development. Whether they go on to have sexual relationships and children in the future or not, it's important that young people grow in their appreciation of their bodies and in their capacity to assert sexual choices, understanding the impact of those choices on their reproductive health and sexual well-being.

Some young people in our churches will already be sexually active. In a later chapter, we consider issues around sexual safety. But for now, let's assume this is consenting sexual activity between two similar-aged young people both over the age of sixteen. One of our roles as youth workers is to encourage and support young people to talk with their parents or carers about sexual activity, having an STI, pregnancy, etc. Sometimes, I've been with young people as they've done exactly this, and we've gone for a walk around the block to give their parents or carers time to think about their response. As online grooming and child sexual exploitation has increased over the years, I've noticed that some parents in churches are more likely to be concerned about the exploitative nature of an unequal sexual relationship than simply if their son or daughter is in a consensual sexual relationship with someone of a similar age. Even as attitudes change, it's still true that most young people in church feel anxious about their parents finding out about their sexual activity, and most Christian parents would prefer their children to delay sexual activity until they are older and in a committed or marriage relationship. Because of this desire for their children's sexual, emotional and spiritual well-being, some Christian parents can find it hard to see supporting their young person to access sexual health information and services as anything other than encouraging them to have sex.

There is a big difference between helping a young person to access accurate information about sex and parents leaving a condom lying around in the hope that if their daughter or son is having sex at least she or he will do it safely. The former is about facilitating good conversation that leads a young person to making informed choices and keeps the door open for ongoing conversation. The latter is a poor substitute for support and isn't based on any evidence that it works. In fact, young people I've worked with whose parents have taken this approach have felt pressure from their parents to begin having sex. We are not honouring Jesus or young people if we avoid uncomfortable conversations or prevent them from knowing the facts and making their own choices. This is why, wherever possible, positive relationships between the parents/guardians and the youth worker is so important for the sexual well-being of young people in our churches.

Both UK law and professional guidance are clear that all young people, including those under the age of thirteen, have the right to access sexual health services and are entitled to confidentiality. Consent from parents or legal guardians is not always legally necessary if it would not be in the young person's best interest and the young person understands the information and has the capacity to consent. The General Medical Council found that:

A confidential sexual health service is essential for the welfare of children and young people. Concern about confidentiality is the biggest deterrent to young people asking for sexual health advice. That in turn presents dangers to young people's own health and to that of the community, particularly other young people.[1]

More for you to consider

- How will you support young people in your church to find out about and be confident to access local, youth-friendly sexual health services? Sometimes, these are based in a secondary school or local community centre. Many chemists have walk-in areas for young people to access contraceptive advice and services. Check whether your area has an 'in the post' home STI testing service.
- It's important to offer information about the menstrual cycle and access to free menstrual products. Your church or youth group could make up good-quality menstrual care bags for girls which could include menstrual products, an information leaflet, clean underwear, a bar of chocolate, body wash, etc. Ask the girls what they would

like in them. Remember to talk with boys about the menstrual cycle. Remember that a trans boy who has not medically transitioned will still be experiencing a menstrual cycle and could need support to access menstrual products.

- How will you create space for conversations about masturbation hygiene and support for young people accessing online porn and erotic literature? This is for boys and girls, although it's often best to have these chats in single-gender (if appropriate) or one-to-one settings.

- How will you make information around STIs and sexual reproduction available to young people in your church? With all the important single-agenda topics (like CSE, FGM, identity politics, sexual violence against girls and women) receiving more of a platform in school PSHE/RSE (personal, social, health and economic education/relationships and sex education) lessons or online, it's important that we don't fail to inform young people about the basics of sexual reproduction and sexual health.

- How will you bust some myths and correct any misinformation around how a male or female body 'should' look at the different stages of puberty? Porn presents an unrealistic and dehumanizing ideal that has nothing to do with healthy sexual development. The more that young people's ideas about their bodies are rooted in reality and a culture of theologically informed body positivity, the more they'll be able to push back against the lies in culture and be advocates for healthy body image.

Exploring the How

Helping young people explore ways to care for their bodies and their sexual health

Self-care has become a popular buzz phrase meaning anything from having a bath to splashing out on a new pair of trainers. It can make us a bit suspicious of it. But self-care is a great skill for young people to develop during puberty, not least because body odour is one of the first signs of puberty. The increase in pre-teen hormonal activity causes the apocrine glands to mature, resulting in increased sweat under the arms and around the groin area.

I know a young person who, the moment she began puberty, refused to have baths or take showers. Eventually, she was able to explain to an adult she trusted that this was because she was feeling anxious about the changes to her body (breast buds growing, under-arm and vaginal odour), so she pretended none of it was happening. Conversations with young people about some very simple and practical ways that they can look after their bodies are really important. It's a good time to reinforce messages about the importance of privacy and their right to have privacy as they wash, get dressed, etc.

Although the prophet Elijah was no longer a teenager when this incident happened, I love the emphasis in the story on practical bodily care after the intensity of spiritual warfare in his fight against the prophet of Baal!

> Suddenly an angel shook him awake and said, 'Get up and eat!'
> He looked around and, to his surprise, right by his head were a loaf of bread baked on some coals and a jug of water. He ate the meal and went back to sleep.
> The angel of GOD came back, shook him awake again, and said, 'Get up and eat some more – you've got a long journey ahead of you.'
> (1 Kings 19.5–7)

Young people need to be able to understand their physical (and emotional) needs and find appropriate and responsible ways to meet those needs – including speaking up for themselves if others transgress their boundaries. Youth workers can accidently reinforce unhelpful stereotypes about puberty. Making jokes about 'smelly teenagers' doesn't help create puberty positivity. This is a brilliant opportunity for close working with the children's workers in the church. It can be an uphill battle to try to be positive about puberty with an eleven-year-old who has already had two years of dealing with puberty jokes and body shaming at school or in their peer group.

There is a misconception in youth culture that sex is an issue that only affects young people. Although the onset of puberty and societal pressures to become sexually active kick in during adolescence, sex is something that people can engage with throughout their lives. Developing heathy habits around sexual health as a young person sets them up well for a life of good sexual health. Instilling practices of self-care in the lives of the young people we serve is part of our calling. They have a long journey towards sexual maturity and well-being in front of them that requires them to be fully embodied in their choices and behaviours. Developing ways to care for their own bodies will equip them with empathy in the care of other people's bodies in future friendships and relationships.

More for you to consider

- In the western Christian faith tradition (and social culture at large), we have lost the art of the rite of passage that marks a child moving into adulthood. How might your church or youth group reconsider the celebration of puberty without falling back on limiting gender stereotypes? Rather than celebrating girls' purity and innocence and boys' bravery, think about celebrating a young person's courage, story, character and potential in a way that is unique to each one.
- How can you encourage positive self-esteem? What could help a young person to appreciate and care for themselves physically? What habits might they need to develop (regularly washing, changing clothes more frequently than they currently do, etc.) that will help them to feel confident in looking after their changing bodies?
- As well as in your one-to-one conversations, how can you help facilitate a culture of body positivity in your family, youth group or church? Are you noticing that young people are being picked on or bullied because of their appearance, smell, spots, voice changing, etc.?
- Social media encourages young people to make public what is private. How can you help young people to develop healthy social media practices, especially around personal images? This might include helping them explore the consequences and impact of 'over-sharing' images they may later regret sharing, or dealing with attention (negative and positive) from people.
- How would you know that a young person is needing support around aspects of puberty? Who else in the church could you draw in? As well as going through your safer recruitment process, think about what training and support you would offer them.

Exploring the Why

Supporting young people to dig deeper into how their sexual health fits into the bigger picture of living with God at the centre of their lives

Sexual reproduction possibly feels like the least 'spiritual' of the five topics we're considering. In many ways it's the most obviously physical: what do menstrual cycles and erections have to do with a young person's discipleship? Everything. We are not ambient souls that happen to have bodies. We are a wonderful integration of body, soul, mind and strength. Learning to care for our physical and sexual health is a way we honour the God who made us and makes his home in us.

There are many reasons why it's good for young people to take care of their sexual reproductive health, and one of them is to do with having babies. Not all young people dream about having babies, but many of them may, when they are older, want to begin a family. Sometimes, infertility is caused by an STI contracted through unprotected sex being left untreated. Two common bacterial STIs (chlamydia and gonorrhoea) that can cause this complication have been on the rise for the last decade and show no signs of slowing down.*** Making positive and informed choices in their teenage years about their sexual activity can increase their chances of being able to have a family later on.

Learning to appreciate and take care of our bodies and sexual health during adolescence is also important to young people's sexual well-being in that any conversation we want to open up with them about sexual safety, sexual desire, sexual intimacy and sexual integrity will be built on this foundation. If young people believe that their bodies are shameful or that their physiological responses to sexual stimuli are sinful, they will find it much harder to accept that their safety, their desires, their longing for intimacy and their lives of integrity are all part of their journey of maturing in faith. The tragedy of this is that young followers of Jesus might not have casual sex in their teenage years but are at risk of internalizing damaging ideas about their sexual selves. As a result, they might find sexual intimacy in the future painful and difficult. This has too often been the untold story in churches. But this doesn't need to be the case. Open, kind,

---

*** STIs can cause a range of complications, infertility being one of them. It's important that the way we talk about STIs doesn't contribute to stigma. Anyone can contract an STI through sexual contact with someone who has an STI.

informed and grace-filled conversations with you can prevent that from happening.

More for you to consider

- Think about encouraging a young person to create a long-term vision for their sexual health. This works better with older teenagers, but a simpler version of it could be beneficial for younger youth. The idea is to help them consider what good sexual health over the span of their lifetime might look like. You could draw a timeline and ask them to write along it key relational events that depict how they would like their life to pan out. It could include meeting someone, having children, fostering, etc. It's entirely up to the young people what they want to contribute. You could ask some prompting questions like: When does someone know they are ready to have sex? When might someone stop having sex and why? Is it possible for elderly people to have healthy sex lives? Why might someone choose to only have one sexual partner throughout a lifetime, or no sexual partners?
- How could you inspire young people to dig deeper into what their experience of their sexual development is showing them about God? Think about how you could help them talk with God about masturbation, changes in their bodies, mood swings – all that comes with going through puberty.

9

The safety thing

Back in the early 2000s, much of the focus around young people's sexual safety was to do with the physical consequences of unprotected sex, in particular STIs. One school in an area with high rate of STIs among young people invited me and a sexual health nurse to speak to each year group about risky sexual behaviour and how to practise safer sex. At the start of each session, I'd surreptitiously find four willing volunteers, two who would let me spray perfume on the palm of one of their hands and two who would agree to keep their hands in their pockets for the duration of the exercise. Then I'd ask all the young people in the hall to stand up, move among each other and shake hands. They would do this – a little sheepishly at first, but then with a lot of noise and enthusiasm. After a few minutes, I'd blow a whistle, which they knew meant they had to stop where they were. Then I would ask them to smell their hand. This took a lot of persuading, but eventually they'd give their palm a quick sniff.

'It smells rank!' someone would invariably shout.

'It's perfume,' I'd explain. 'Who else can smell perfume on their hand?' Most of the hands would go up. Then I'd ask the two people who were the source of the perfume to come to the front. 'Who remembers shaking these people's hands?' I'd ask. Fewer would put their hands up. 'So if you didn't shake one of these people's hands, how is it that your hand smells of the perfume that I only sprayed on their hands?'

Then I'd ask for anyone who couldn't smell perfume on their hand to come to the front. The two students who were asked to stuff their hands in their pockets for the activity would shuffle forward. 'Why do the rest of you think these guys didn't get "infected" with perfume?' I'd ask.

A wise kid would always pipe up, 'Because they were wearing a condom, miss!'

'*And* choosing to only shake each other's hand!' someone would add, hopefully.

Albeit in a clunky way, we wanted to show these young people that it's not only *their own* choices about sex that put them at risk of an STI, but also the choices of the people they have sex with. One girl described it as 'a sexy family tree'. I'm not sure how helpful a description that is, but she was on the right track. Having unprotected sex (sex without a condom) with person A who has had unprotected sex with two people who've both had unprotected sex with two other people means that your sexual experience with person A involves the sexual history of at least seven people.

The importance of knowing a partner's sexual history isn't limited to sexually active teenagers. In a survey of 2,000 adults in the UK, 22 per cent of the respondents (the highest number) said they have had sex with between five and nine other people. Just 3 per cent reported zero sexual partners and 1 per cent reported having up to ninety sexual partners.[1] Any sexual activity with someone who has been sexually active with someone else can put you at risk of infection. It's interesting how little we hear these significant sexual health messages today.

When we think about young people's sexual safety today, I wonder how high STIs are on our list of priorities. We're more likely to think about sexual exploitation, peer-on-peer sexual abuse and partner or dating violence than we are young people getting pregnant or genital herpes – and there are serious reasons for this. Gender-based aggression and sexual violence against girls are on the rise in youth culture. A website founded by 22-year-old Soma Sara in 2021 invited teenage girls to share their stories of the 'rape culture' they claimed is prevalent in UK schools. One young person wrote that she was 'regularly sexually harassed and groped by boys at school in front of teachers that "turned a blind eye". One of these boys went on to assault me and another raped me. I never reported any of it, I was too ashamed.'[2] One mother writes that her thirteen-year-old daughter was:

being touched inappropriately by a boy in her year . . . It was fairly minor touching – on the back and the shoulder – but he was doing it in a suggestive way, stroking her and things like that. It was unwelcome and she made it clear that it was unwelcome. But he didn't stop.

Instead, he made sexual remarks, telling her, 'You make me hard.'

Another parent commented, after her teenage daughter received an anonymous photo of a man's erect penis and an offer to pay her for oral sex, 'I was quite shocked, but . . . she and her friends seem to have stopped even thinking about it as a problem.'[3]

Asked for his view of whether teenage boys are doing this because they think girls want it, one young man replied, 'I don't think that boys even think about it. It's just so prevalent.'[4]

How is it that, in a post #MeToo world, young people are growing up in a culture where teenage boys sexually assaulting teenage girls is 'prevalent'? The DFID Guidelines for addressing the social norms that lead to violence against women and girls, states:

> Violence is often, although not always, a part of dominant constructions of masculinity in many societies. If there are social expectations that men control women, then physical and sexual force are often seen as 'legitimate' ways to exert this control. This control also extends to punishment and sanction of those who resist, rebel or transgress gender norms . . . This helps to explain why men are the primary perpetrators of violence and why women are so often the victims, but also why sexual minorities are frequently the victims of gender violence.[5]

One place where young people receive messages about men controlling women is through online porn. Even young people who don't access porn or erotic literature are in peer groups of young people who do. Analysis of scenes from best-selling online porn videos found that 90 per cent of scenes contained sexual aggression against women who either showed neutrality or pleasure in response to the violence.[6] Young people who watch porn are witnessing violent sexual actions against girls and women that are demonstrated, glorified, repeated and encouraged in this intense, sexually arousing, behaviour-shaping and permission-giving experience.

Conversations about sexual safety are about supporting young people to be sexually safe, whether that's online, in relationships or in their social groups. They're also about inspiring young people to challenge damaging cultural norms and advocate for change, as well as encouraging them to relate to each other with deep respect and compassion.

Safe to grow

Safety is one of our most basic needs. Without a sense of being safe, young people can't take the positive risks that help them explore their world and build resilience to help them cope with life's challenges. When young people don't feel safe, all their energy is directed to fight or flight. Without safety, there is no growth.

Young people's safety is a huge priority to God. He tasks us with protecting the vulnerable (Proverbs 24.11–12), speaking up against violence, equipping young people with tools to establish healthy practices to enable themselves to be and feel safe, and advocating for a safer society where everyone can flourish.

> One important sign that shalom is present in a society is evidence that public space is safe sexual space. To the extent to which a person, female or male, feels sexually unsafe while participating in the various arenas of life, to that extent shalom is absent.[7]

Being aware of the potential for sexual harm might prompt a panic-induced response in us. It's not surprising that we seek to keep young people from any situation where they may be at increased risk of sexual pressure or exploitation. There will indeed be times when we need to step in to protect young people. In the course of a conversation with a young person you may see or notice things that give you cause for concern. You should already be aware of your own church or organization's safeguarding policy and be familiar with the process of reporting concerns. There will be someone who is designated to fulfil the role of safeguarding lead who will have received training and will know who to report concerns to.[8]

But as well as being vigilant for signs of coercion and abuse,[9] we can arm young people with guidance and skills to identify and assess risk to minimize sexual harm in the situations they are in. One challenge is to talk about being sexually safe without over-emphasizing sexual harm. As the teenage brain is more prone to downplaying risk and overstating the potential gains of the gamble, labelling all risk-taking behaviour as harmful and telling young people not to do something risky doesn't remove the desire to do it. In fact, it might make it more appealing. If we want young people to curb risky behaviours that could harm themselves or others, we need to highlight the gains of being safe. Youth culture tends to promote recklessness as a badge of honour and safety as a sign of being boring. But it takes true courage to be safe and to promote the safety and well-being of others. Our focus needs to be on painting a compelling vision of the power of taking good risks that promote well-being and growth.

David Wright, Director of the UK Safer Internet Centre, lays out the challenge for educators:

A school year group is shown a video on online safety and often it's about extreme harm online with the pretext that if we show young people what harm looks like, they will be able to recognise it when they see it. But when we learn how to drive, we don't just watch clips of car crashes to learn how to do it. The current approach makes massive assumptions that children are able to contextualise what they see.[10]

Whenever we talk about sexual safety, we're not just focusing on all the things that are harmful to us and others. We want to be talking about the good risks we are prepared to take and how positive experimentation with the world around us can build young people's resilience, resourcefulness and creativity in how they live well and seek to bring about positive change for others.

So let's look at how we can help young people explore the what, how and why questions around sexual safety.

Exploring the What

Considering what young people want and need to know about being safe

A place to start is discerning what the young people's most pressing needs are in terms of their sexual safety. Are they taking too many uncalculated risks? Are they in situations where they 'feel' safe but are not safe? Maybe they're not taking enough risks because they see all physical activity (including kissing and hugging) as sinful or shameful behaviour. If they are sexually active, how are they reducing the risks of pregnancy and STIs? Is it consensual, and do they understand what makes sexual activity consensual and safer?

A good rule of thumb in helping young people understand sexual safety is to provide them with information, not rules. There will, of course, be important information that includes rules, such as the law around sexual consent and the sharing of explicit images and material. But you want to avoid telling young people what they should or shouldn't do. Instead, focus on helping them to explore accurate information.

Safer sex

There are many different types of sexual activity, some carrying a higher risk of contracting infection than others. Anal sex carries the greatest risk of passing on infections such as HIV and hepatitis, followed by vaginal sex and then oral sex. Safer sex means having sex with less risk of unwanted pregnancy and STIs. Other types of sexual activity, like fingering or fisting, carry a very low risk of spreading infection, but the risk of infection increases if either person has any cuts or broken skin that come into contact with their partner.

If you're in conversation with young people who are engaging in sexual activity (even if it's 'just oral sex'), it's important that they lower the risk of contracting an STI and pregnancy (in the case of vaginal sex or fingering) by proper use of condoms made of latex or polyurethane, not made from natural materials as these have a short shelf life and don't currently protect against STIs. Good communication with their partner as well as with a sexual health nurse contributes to reducing the risk of pregnancy and STIs.

Safer relationships

Any sexual activity is only as safe as the relationship. Being able to trust each other and communicate well is essential to being able to negotiate challenges and build a safe, equal relationship. Shared values are a strong foundation for a safe relationship, especially if one of those values is seeking to grow in relationship with God.

Although it's not the case that going out with another Christian automatically makes for an equal and safe relationship, it's important for young people to consider how going out with someone who might not share their values or beliefs about sex might influence them. If the young people feel that their church may react negatively to them seeing a non-Christian, they are more likely to be secretive or unsure how to seek support from you, which could make them more vulnerable.

Sexual consent

Sexual consent means actively agreeing to sexual activity with someone and letting them know that the activity is wanted. Most films and TV series don't model this. Instead, young people see a couple going from chatting in the bar to having sex. The steps in between are mostly absent. The only way to know if someone is consenting to sex (or any physical or sexual contact) is if they explicitly say they want it. This includes within marriage. If in doubt as to whether someone is consenting or not, assume that they're not.

Saying 'no'

The only completely safe sex is no sex, which is a positive option. Contrary to what young people may be told through mass media, friendships and relationships don't require sexual activity to deepen an emotional bond. Saying no isn't a negation of love or intimacy. Sexual activity can bring a level of risk that young people are not ready for, and that can put a heavy strain on them. Delaying sexual activity, particularly penetrative sexual activity, is a positive health choice for young people and frees them up to enjoy less risky, loving physical contact, such as kissing, hugging and holding hands.

Young people may find that when they say 'no' to sexual activity, their peers or partner might want to know why, which is understandable. But no one should ever be forced to give a reason for their answer, especially if they don't feel safe to do so. 'No' is always enough.

Sometimes, it might not be clear to a young person that they are unsafe or what they need to say no to. It's important that we can help them to define what is meant by unwanted attention or inappropriate sexual behaviour from another person. Don't just say, 'Inappropriate touching is unacceptable.' Think about how you could define it. 'A boy stroking a girl's bum as she walks past him at school is inappropriate behaviour.' 'A girl sitting on a boy's lap at youth club and wiggling around to make his friends laugh is inappropriate behaviour.' In what other ways might the young people want to define it? I sometimes use words like 'behaviour or language that makes you or another person feel uncomfortable', while recognizing that it's not always easy for a young person to identify these feelings. A young person in love (dopamine flooding their brain) may struggle to see that the pressure or violence they're experiencing from their partner is harmful, unacceptable behaviour and not 'what people who are in love do'.

More for you to consider

- Think about whether you need to pass on any concerns to your safeguarding lead. Who else could you signpost the young people to for ongoing support?
- If as a result of your conversation young people choose to establish new boundaries around sexual activity or behaviour in their relationships, what sort of ongoing support might they need? For some, telling a partner that they don't want to have sex any more could mean the end of that relationship, which could be devastating for them.
- As well as helping the young person define what is and isn't acceptable sexual behaviour, help them think about the myths around sexual consent and why they're not true. If a girl is wearing a short skirt, does that mean she's 'up for it'? Is sexual assault an act of lust or passion that's just gone a bit wrong? If someone doesn't fight back when they're being verbally abused, groped or assaulted, does that mean they want it?
- What training might you benefit from accessing?

Exploring the How

Helping young people explore ways to be safe and to contribute to sexually safe environment, peer groups and relationships

A lot of the positive behaviours we want to encourage in young people are caught, not taught. So what could it mean for you to influence a young person's behaviour rather than seek to control what they do, where they go and who they see? This begins with modelling a safe relationship in how you relate to them. It also means paying attention to how you and the team contribute to a sexually safe environment at the youth group and the wider church. This will include setting clear guidelines with the young people (and all adults who work with them) about acceptable and unacceptable behaviour. Think about the relationships that are modelled to the young people in your church and youth programmes – are they mutually respectful and safe? Do adult leaders model kindness and vulnerability in how they interact with each other and the young people? Are the young people able to talk openly about sexual risks, and are their questions, needs, concerns and disclosures treated sensitively and effectively? Do you recognize and respond to the particular vulnerability of young people with reference to their past experiences, additional needs, trauma and other emotional needs?

When dealing with risky situations, young people often choose behaviours that are consequence free, like secrecy or lying. This is often because the feelings of shame can be too much to face. Being a person of influence in a young person's life depends on you being easy for them to turn to and spend time with. They won't let their guard down and face what's happening if they feel that you will try to control the situation, shame them or tell them what to do.

More for you to consider

- In practice, how will you seek to be a positive influence in the young people's lives, rather than seek to exercise control over their risk-taking behaviours? Think about how you will make it easy for them to open up to you and feel safe with you.
- If you do need to raise concerns with your safeguarding lead, how will you do this in a way that still keeps this young person at the centre of decisions made about them?
- Think about how you will support young people who are vulnerable to sexual harm as a result of previous experiences, low self-worth, etc. to explore how they are deeply loved by God.
- How will you challenge either high-risk behaviours or not enough risk taking?

- How could you help the young people know if someone is putting emotional or sexual pressure on them? As well as exploring what they could do in those situations, help them to think about what other things they could do to keep themselves safe (i.e., do they know other people at the party? Do they know how they will get home? What effect could drinking alcohol or using drugs have on their capacity to assess risk and keep themselves safe?)

Exploring the Why

Supporting young people to dig deeper into how being sexually safe fits into the bigger picture of living with God at the centre of their lives

If you are of a certain age, you will no doubt have used the legendary soft-drink can illustration. For the uninitiated, it goes like this. Drill a hole in the bottom of a can and drain out the liquid. Don't open it using the pull ring, so that the can looks unopened when in fact it is empty. Then get two young people to have a competition to see who can crush a can with their bare hands. Give one young person the full can and the other the empty one. It doesn't take a genius to work out what happens next. It works best if you give the regular can to a young person with a bit of muscle and the empty can (which is easy to crush) to a much younger teenager. The point is that it's what's inside that makes you strong, not how tough you look.

It's difficult to live vulnerably in a culture that often shames weakness and where kindness is seen as a failing. For all young people, developing an alternative view of being strong and powerful is essential to being able to live sexually safe lives. If it's what they're being filled with that gives young people strength to resist the pressure, we need to help them decide what they're going to be filled with. As important as they are, strategies and skills are not enough.

It's not for nothing that Jesus chose young disciples who abounded in risk-taking behaviours to be the carriers of the gospel. He saw hunger and raw potential in them. I can't help but smile at the thought of Jesus choosing people who he knew would totally try out all the stuff he said they'd be able to do in his name: crush snakes, walk on water, raise the dead, heal the sick, go to the ends of the earth.

As well as equipping young people to feel and be safe, we want to draw them out into choppy waters where they discover how to live courageously and sacrificially for the sake of others. Being a person who others are sexually, physically and emotionally safe to be with is a mark of Christian discipleship. The fruit of a deeper reverence for God is a deeper reverence for other people. Gaining this perspective allows us to truly see other people as they really are, not as people who are there to meet our needs or do what we want them to do. The Spirit of God at work in young people's lives shows up not only in their self-control (among other things!) but also in their faithfulness in caring for others and in their goodness in speaking out against injustice and behaviours, worldviews, attitudes and environments that cause harm.

Paul's words to the church in Ephesus ring true for us: 'Behave as children of light. Light has its fruit, doesn't it, in everything that's good and just and true. Think through what's going to be pleasing to the Lord. Work it out' (Ephesians 5.8–10, NTE). Ancient Greek culture, much like ours today, saw no need for sexual restraint. It wasn't a sexually safe place to be. 'Those who were enlightened could do what they wanted with their bodies; it was people who were still in the dark who thought they had to practise restraint.'[11] When Paul encourages us to 'behave as children of light', he's flipping the cultural narrative on its head. He's saying that, when we follow Christ, we don't just become enlightened people; we also become the light that shines brightly in the darkness. Not having sex with a partner we're not married to and resisting by speaking out against damaging sexual norms that hurt people are ways in which we live in the light and carry the light.

10

The desire thing

Desire often gets a bad press. Particularly adolescent desire. If only young people didn't *want* stuff, didn't obsess about fitting in or having what everyone else has. If only they had more self-control, they would be spared (and would spare us) a whole load of grief and mess.

I spend a lot of time standing in skate parks. It's one of the only places where my nine-year-old and three-year-old children feel equally happy, scooting up ramps and sliding back down half pipes. Groups of young teenagers move around the park. I watch them, rolling in like waves on the beach. At this age, gender isn't personal; it's tribal. Girls in black leggings, phones in hand, eyes on the boys, fixed to other girls at the elbow, swarm as one being around the edges of the half pipes. Some boys form the 'serious-skater' cartel, dominating the space with their leaps and tricks. At first glance, they look like they're in charge. But there's another group of lads, the ones without the knee pads and scooters, hovering on the opposite side to the girls, filling the space with dark looks and loud cusses. Then, of course, there are always one or two young people going it alone, but among young teens in a skate park on a Saturday afternoon, these precious few are the outliers. The anomalies.

Give it a few years and *all* these young people will be more diverse in their friendships across the gender binary, more able to tolerate differences, more confident in communication, more able to hold their own. But right now, they are who their group says they are. They want what their group wants. They mimic, so they are. But this mimicry is about more than just surviving. They want to fit in with their tribe (belonging), but they also want to stand out (purpose) among their tribe as the one who epitomizes who it is they are all craving to be.

René Girard, the French literary theorist and philosopher of social sciences, wrote extensively about desire. He believed that, although everyone holds firmly to the authentic nature of their own desires, the fact is that our desires are shaped by our social environment. In essence, we want what other people want. We want it because other people want it. And we don't only *want* what other people want; we also want to *be* the person whose desires everyone emulates. This is how consumerism works. The most effective adverts are those that show you the kind of person who wants the product you're being sold. 'You should want to be like them, because, well, look at them! Who wouldn't want to be them? And now you can, when you buy [insert product].'

Fyre Festival, the fraudulently marketed luxury music festival on the Bahamian island of Great Exuma in 2017, was an example of this. Young adults parted with eye-watering sums of money to be part of the greatest party – which never happened. But what got them splashing their cash were social media feeds full of supermodels 'at' the festival, frolicking in crystal blue waters on white sandy beaches, living their best life 'on the boundaries of the impossible'.[1] The subtle message was, 'You too can be like them, live like them, hang out with them, be desired like them. It's just one ticket and plane ride away.'

Our desires are constantly under the influence of external forces. This knowledge can lead us to one of two conclusions: either we think all our desires must be met, or we see all desire as inherently bad. For the former, denial is the greatest sin. If you want it (and it's legal), then you can have it. Freedom is having what you want, when you want. For the latter, the sin is in the wanting. Desires are so fickle and can lead to such destructive places that freedom is feeling no desire at all. Many churches lean towards this view. If desire is bad per se, then life without desire is the desired state.

I hope the irony isn't lost on you.

We can only desire a life that is *not* at the mercy of our desires if we first accept that, as a motivation in our lives, desire is a good thing. Without it, we wouldn't search for God because we wouldn't have the hunger to know him. As René Girard, himself a convert to Christianity in later life, said, 'Desire is not of this world . . . it is in order to penetrate into another world that one desires; it is in order to be initiated into a radically foreign existence.'[2]

The heart of desire

Desire has a powerful role to play in our lives. It's the 'precious clue that ever tugs at the heart, reminding the human soul – however dimly – of its created source'.[3] Desire is good and intrinsic to our created design. We have a strong relational attraction for God that goes beyond our understanding of sexual longing and desire. You could say that there's a lusting after God that is life-giving. 'A white-tailed deer drinks from the creek; I want to drink God, deep drafts of God. I'm thirsty for God-alive' (Psalm 42.1–2).

We're also creatures who are desired by the Divine:

'Israel, out looking for a place to rest,
met God out looking for them!'
God told them, 'I've never quit loving you and never will.
Expect love, love, and more love!'
(Jeremiah 31.2–3)

Although we don't always see what we desire most, we experience shadows, hints, pulls, nudges in our desires to crave something more. To desire is to be human. Early church father St Augustine, who had some spectacularly terrible ideas about female sexuality, wrote some inspired things about desire. It's a reminder that someone can be brilliant and flawed at the same time!

The entire life of a good Christian is an exercise in holy desire. You do not see what you long for, but the very act of desiring prepares you, so that when God comes you may see and be utterly satisfied. Suppose you are going to fill some holder or container, and you know you will be given a large amount. Then you set about stretching your sack or wineskin or whatever it is. Why? Because you know the quantity you will have to put in it, and your eyes tell you there is not enough room. By stretching it, therefore, you increase the capacity of the sack and this is how God deals with us. Simply by making us wait God increases our desire, which in turn enlarges the capacity of our soul, making it able to receive what is to be given to us.[4]

Any desire met in the wrong way can lead us away from Jesus. But our desires can be the strongest forces to lead us towards him. Imagine if we understood adolescent sexual desire within this broader framework of longing for God. Appreciating, examining and being intentional in how we express sexual desire is vital for everyone, and particularly for young people who are doing this in relation to God. In reflecting on becoming aware of his sexual desires as a young gay man, my friend Luke makes this observation: 'My sexuality has been the thing that has brought me back to Jesus, time and time again. I now rejoice in the deeper elements of having to wrestle with that, because it kept showing me God's grace.' It's important that any young person has the chance to discover more of God's grace in the midst of their growing awareness of sexual responses and desires.

Deeper desire

Our identity comes from being the objects of God's desire. But the contemporary idea that we are what we desire is a mark of a consumer culture that has been carried into our understanding of our sexuality. There will be young people in your church who will be experiencing sexual or romantic attractions for people of the same or both sexes. How a young person self-identifies matters, and it's important that, irrespective of identity labels or sexual desires, they receive the unconditional love and welcome of their church family. Like all desire, sexual desires can evolve. Sometimes they contradict each other and sometimes they mask a deeper longing. In supporting young people to explore what their sexual attractions mean for them, we need to make the link between sexual desires and sexual identity with care.

A survey by YouGov found that 48 per cent of respondents aged 18-24 saw themselves as exclusively heterosexual.[5] This is compared to 78 per cent of the respondents aged between 55 and 75 years old. Does this mean that young people are more likely to be gay or bisexual? British political writer and gay rights activist Matthew Parris asks whether there is more pressure on young people to 'exaggerate their sexual versatility' when a society becomes more accepting of sexual diversity:

We are herd animals; we need to admit that peer-group pressure can play a significant role as an unconscious modular of sexuality, and not to be too quick to interpret every youthful assertion of same-sex attraction as some sacred expression of a person's true self.[6]

The only way to know whether a young person will be a straight, gay or bisexual adult is to wait to see if they are a straight, gay or bisexual adult. Parris' comment is a reminder that, as sexual attractions develop during adolescence, it's important to give a young person space and support as they journey with their sexuality.

Sexual desires are important, but they aren't the only or main defining thing about young people's identity. Ironically, churches tend to agree with this until young people in their church come out as gay or tell someone they're experiencing sexual feelings for someone of the same sex. When that happens, we can be guilty of reducing their identity to their sexual desires and either 'agree' with them or 'disagree' with them. I hope that no church is actually saying that a gay or trans person is a non-person. But what happens is that, in these instances, we tend to make the mistake of over-emphasizing the sexual feelings that could lead to behaviours seen as not in line with their faith identity, rather than supporting the young people to see the potential for their desires, even ones that make them feel confused or that their church finds uncomfortable, to lead them to God.

Young people are not being sinful in experiencing same-sex sexual desires, any more than young people are being sinful in experiencing opposite-sex sexual desires. But teenagers who are experiencing sexual desire in ways that are incongruous with their church's teaching on sexuality are more likely to experience intense feelings of shame, guilt and self-hatred. Most LGBTQ+ teenagers will have thought and wrestled with understanding and untangling their sexual desires to a level that 'normative' heterosexual young people may not have.

Although churches respond differently to how and when these sexual desires can be acted upon (depending on their conviction of a biblical sexual ethic), it's vitally important that, first and foremost, young people are listened to and accepted with love and grace. Sexual feelings aren't a barrier to the love of God and the power of the Spirit. As followers of Jesus, we are *all* called to celibacy outside marriage. The discipleship 'issue' isn't whether a young person's sexual desires are same sex, opposite sex or bisexual. Discipleship creates the space for *all* young people to examine their desires and how they might best express them in line with their beliefs and values.

So let's look at how we can help a young person explore the what, how and why questions around sexual desire.

Exploring the What

Considering what young people want and need to understand about desire

God equipped our bodies with hormones, so it's a good idea to get to know the role that some of these play in our experience of desire.

Our brain is the control centre that releases the two primary sex hormones in the body: testosterone and oestrogen. Both hormones are essential in the creation of desire. Scientists believe that a combination of testosterone and oestrogen is the ultimate love drug. This is because these two sex hormones stimulate neurochemicals in the brain such as dopamine, serotonin, norepinephrine and oxytocin. The mash-up of these neurochemicals triggers dizzying feelings of excitement and passion. They're what we're feeling when we talk about 'falling in love' or when we're turned on sexually. We're literally being driven to distraction by a fire in our body! It's worth spending more time with these neurochemicals because they're amazing.

- Dopamine. We mostly talk about dopamine in the context of addiction and drug dependency. It's the neurotransmitter that makes the things we see, hear or do arousing. It associates feeling pleasure and satisfaction with certain things or actions. It's also what's released into our brain whenever we encounter something or someone we associate these pleasurable feelings with.
- Serotonin is the neurotransmitter that teaches our bodies a cycle of desire and satisfaction.
- Norepinephrine is the neurotransmitter that's stimulated when we need an extra surge of energy to escape a scary or dangerous situation. It also increases during any sexual activity. It peaks and declines after orgasm.
- Oxytocin is often referred to as the bonding drug. It lowers our defences and strengthens our bonds. Although it's different from

the other neurotransmitters in that it doesn't stimulate arousal, it is essential in the experience of desire.

But even with all the science at our fingertips, desire is a profound mystery. Feelings of sexual desire can happen incredibly quickly and often under the radar of conscious thought; we don't always know quite what it is that turns us on.

For teenagers experiencing these sexual responses for the first time, it's important that they are reminded that desire is essentially good, even if the reason they want to talk is because they're experiencing complicated feelings around their desires. A good starting point is for them to see how not all desires that present as sexual are about sex (or *just* about sex). As an example, masturbation, which is often about dealing with sexual arousal, can also be about the deeper need to feel loved, or needing a sense of power. Understanding what might lie behind the obvious desire to masturbate could be a fruitful avenue of conversation for a young person. By not responding with, 'You need to stop it, now!' you're opening up the opportunity for a young person to tap into any deeper desire that might lie behind this behaviour.

Although during the teenage years, for a lot of young people, sexual behaviour is limited to masturbation, it's really common for girls and boys to start to experiment with sexual arousal through flirting, hugging, hitting each other, tickling, 'making out', etc. A lot of this can be in public, in large peer groups, and may not be between young people who are in a couple. Sexual arousal is all about the anticipation of sexual activity, which doesn't mean that, when this begins, young people are suddenly about to start having sex with each other. During adolescence, young people experience physiological responses in their minds and bodies, preparing them for sexual activity in the future. It's important for them to know that this doesn't indicate that they should be having sex or that they're ready to have sex.

Sexual responses don't need to be acted on, now or ever. That's not the same as saying that sexual responses are bad or that young people should ignore the feelings of being turned on. First, that's pretty much an impossible ask, and second, sexual responses are just that – responses to external stimuli. It could be a sex scene in a film, a flash of cleavage, a lingering kiss, explicit lyrics or even nothing in particular. But although we may be sexually aroused by what we see or hear, we don't need to act on them if we're not ready or not wanting to engage in sexual activity. In fact, if we grow up thinking that we need to act on every sexual impulse we have, we don't grow into safe adults who exercise self-control. Freedom, sexual or otherwise, isn't about doing whatever we want because of a sexual response. Sexual freedom is about recognizing when we are aroused and having strategies to channel that into healthy, sexually fulfilling behaviours that are in line with our values and beliefs.

More for you to consider

- What might a young person ask you about sexual desires that you would feel happy and confident to answer? What questions might make you feel nervous or unsure about how to give an answer?
- What do you believe about sexual attraction and desires?
- How could you ensure that a young person identifying as LGBTQ+ or experiencing same-sex sexual attraction is receiving non-judgemental, confidential and loving support in your church or youth group? What might some of the barriers be to that? How could these be overcome?
- What has been your experience of encountering God at your point of overwhelming desire for something that wasn't him, but he used it to connect deeply with you? For example, it could have been your desire for a new job, a partner, a baby . . .

Exploring the How

Helping young people explore ways to understand their sexual responses and desires

Talking about what they're feeling or what they're curious about helps young people explore their sexual responses *without* needing to be sexually active. Sexually explicit material (in music, films, TV series, online porn) and erotic literature is geared towards causing sexual arousal. The problem isn't that young people are feeling sexually aroused, it's what their bodies are programmed to do in response to sexual stimuli. The problem is that often these feelings might happen suddenly and feel confusing, overwhelming or even unwanted. Many young people may feel unsure what to do with these feelings. It can lead to both repressive and excessive behaviours as young people struggle to find healthy and constructive ways to manage them.

We can help young people identify how the things they're watching, reading, listening to or getting involved in are triggering their sexual arousal, as well as practical ways in which they can manage these. We don't need to ask for details about sexual fantasies or ideas these might trigger. The idea is to help them notice how different situations cause a sexual response in their bodies and thoughts so that they can take control of their responding behaviour.

Here are some steps they can take to positively respond to unwanted sexual arousal or sexual responses they are choosing not to pursue:

- Divert – in any given moment, it's possible to close their eyes, switch off, walk away, stop an action or ask another person to stop what they're doing.
- Distract – instead of carrying on engaging with the material, activity or thought that is causing sexual arousal, what alternative positive behaviour could the young people engage in that will produce feel-good pheromones? Go for a run. Paint their nails. Talk with a friend. Play an online game. Kick a football around. Take the dog for a walk. Bake a cake. Hug a friend.
- Delay – if young people have already a developed a habit around a sexual behaviour, it might be a step too far to begin with diverting or distracting techniques. If they can identify when the desire to begin the sexual behaviour begins, they can choose to delay starting that process. For example, if they feel the urge to watch porn the moment they get home from school, could they begin a new habit of making themselves a snack when they get home, or going to the park on the way home? Could they increase the number of things they regularly do between getting home and watching porn? Over time, these delaying tactics can lead to diverting and distracting techniques.
- Devotion – when a young person is feeling sexual arousal that they aren't able to act on or are choosing not to pursue, they can connect with God. Is there a worship song they could listen to, or a passage of Scripture they could memorize to help ground them in God's desire

148

for them and their desire for God? It's important that this *isn't* instead of pursuing practical techniques. But as they pursue these practical responses in the power of the Holy Spirit they will know the love and power of God, equipping them to exercise self-control and know a deeper freedom.

More for you to consider

- What are healthy ways for a young person to learn about and explore their sexual interests and desires?
- What are unhealthy or damaging ways for a young person to learn about and explore their sexual interests and desires?
- How will you respond if young people tell you that they're experimenting with different sexual partners?
- How can you create space for young people to encounter God? How might you need to prepare them for using silence and solitude to draw close to God?
- Name some ways you can you help young people develop habits and practices of tuning in to God's voice so that they learn to do this for themselves.
- How can you help young people to discern the difference between the disapproval of a Christian community and the conviction of the Holy Spirit?

Exploring the Why

Supporting young people to dig deeper into how their desires fit into the bigger picture of living with God at the centre of their lives

A Christian theology of sexual desire has the idea of surrender at its heart. Having whatever we desire sexually doesn't make the experience better. We don't have better sexual experiences because we act on every sexual response we experience. Our desires are ultimately to draw us to God and to each other in self-giving love.

Take monks and nuns. If you were to ask them why they have chosen not to act on sexual desires for another person, they don't tend to use the language of sacrifice and struggle. They use the language of freedom: freedom to love God more recklessly and to love people more inclusively without having to weigh up the need for a spouse or for children. Whether a

149

young person is choosing sexual faithfulness in a relationship or chastity, developing practices of sexual constraint doesn't mean choosing sexual repression. It means choosing what desires they want to fuel and see grow. As young people learn to give themselves to God in surrender, they will discover that they can exercise control over their sexual responses and desires.

There is not a consensus in the Church around the world as to whether sexual activity between people of the same sex is honouring to God. Some Christians believe that, although experiencing sexual attraction and desire for someone of the same sex is not sinful, engaging in a sexual relationship with that person would be. Others would say that sexual activity between two consenting and faithful people of the same sex is defensible from Scripture and that the Church should bless same-sex marriage. Your church will have its own convictions on this issue. It's vital that young people in your church who are exploring their sexuality understand how much they are loved, valued and wanted not only by God, but also by this Christian community.

More for you to consider

- Is this church congregation able to fully support young people in how they understand and express their sexuality? If this is not the case, and if the young people are struggling or suffering as a result, you could help them explore a different Christian community to continue their discipleship. If this does happen, do all you can to communicate love, support and blessing from the church community they are leaving. Continue to pray for them and, if possible and welcomed by the young people, stay in contact with them.

11

The intimacy thing

It was by far the best-attended seminar of the whole conference.

The panel of 'long-in-the-tooth' (and long-in-the-beard for some of them too) youth pastors drew a huge crowd of younger leaders eager to hear the no-holds-barred stories of what it takes to stay in youth ministry. But it wasn't just stories of success they were after. It was stories of failure too. The ones where the person on the platform spoke with courage and vulnerability about the wounds, pains and struggles of leadership. These were moments of profound leaning in, and although most of us didn't know each other, we felt a closeness that made us feel understood.

Have you ever felt that – an affinity with a complete stranger? Jane Austen famously wrote that time on its own doesn't equal intimacy. You could spend five minutes with one person and feel you've always known them, and work with another person for thirty years and still have no idea who they really are. Why is that? *How* is that? Arguably, the greatest gift is having someone in your life that you can share a deep connection with. This could be sexual, but it doesn't need to be. Sexual intimacy is one type of intimacy, but by no means the only, or the most fulfilling. Our lives are richer for having people we share emotional or intellectual intimacy with. There are friends we share experiences and adventures with. We may have people we're physically intimate with as we care for them. Still others we experience a spiritual intimacy with as we pray and worship together.

Whenever I ask young people if they think that sex and intimacy are the same thing, they invariably say no, even if they don't quite get the question.

'What does it meant to get close to someone?' I ask a young person I know.

He explains physical contact. It sounds like sex.

151

'Does this happen between friends?' I ask.

'Friends with benefits,' comes the reply. ('Friends with benefits' is where two people benefit from a relationship where they have sex without any other commitment.)

'So you're saying that intimacy *is* about sex, even if it's not about a relationship?' I clarify.

'Yeah, because you don't need to be in a relationship to have sex with someone,' he replies.

'But could you be with someone, not have sex, and still feel a deep connection with them?' I ask.

For young people growing up in a society that struggles to model healthy, non-sexual intimacy, where do they look for ideas of how this happens?

The ease and speed at which private, intimate moments can be recorded, shared, commented on and saved in today's culture is at an all-time high. Most research shows a smaller percentage of young people reporting taking or sharing nudes than those who have seen nudes. But a message or an image doesn't need to be sexual or include nudity to be intimate. Many young people report feeling more confident to be 'real' online, and, for many young people, digital communication has become the default means of communication. This is clearly significant as, during adolescence, the importance of friendships and romantic or sexual relationships is taken to a completely new level. In a culture that over-emphasizes sexual intimacy at the expense of other ways to experience closeness with another, how do we steer young people towards a greater understanding of their need for intimacy and towards ways to explore this positively?

The God-touch

I was fascinated to discover that touch is the first sense to develop in the womb. All through our lives, positive touch from other people triggers endorphins, those feel-good chemicals that act in the brain to dull pain. When we are starved of touch, our health suffers. Positive interactions with other people strengthen our immune system, lead to a longer life expectancy, lower stress and blood pressure and improve our mental health.

Why is it that our well-being is so tied into our social interactions with each other? Why do we crave intimacy?

The Bible answers that. We crave intimacy because we're made by a God who uniquely created us out of intimacy and for intimacy. Humanity's origin story in Genesis is a far cry from the other creation myths that were doing the rounds in the ancient world. These violent tales of gods at war, producing humans out of destructive impulses and enslaving them to their desire for dominion, are very distant from the story in Genesis. Here is a God who doesn't need raw materials to create life, and who doesn't *need* to create humans to serve a lust for power or support a bruised ego. God is already fulfilled in perfect relationship; totally fulfilled in the intimate union of Father, Son and Spirit. So God creates human beings for one reason and one reason alone: love. Everything that exists does so because God loves it into being.

The cosmos-creating love of God is the basis for our existence and it sets our lives on a trajectory to seek meaningful connection with others. This is why every young person craves intimacy. Being created out of intimate relationship also means they're created *for* intimate relationship. Intimacy is in our design, so no wonder we see such a desire for it in young people. It's also little wonder that it's a hotly contested concept in today's culture – just think of the lies that we're vulnerable to believing about it.

One such lie is that we need to prove our worth in order to be the kind of person another person would want to share any type of intimacy with. Another is that being intimate with someone is just about sex, a lie now backed by the multi-billion-dollar porn industry and mass media. Think about popular music lyrics, plot lines, influencer lifestyles – they all paint an idealistic and unreal picture of intimacy: sexy people in idyllic places having easy, mind-blowing sex. It falsely connects intimacy with perfection, which in turn sows the lie deep into young people's consciousness that they're incomplete unless they're in a perfect relationship. This can lead to shame as they come to believe that they're not the sort of people that anyone would want to get to know. Lies like this can prevent young people from appreciating what intimacy really is, and in turn how they can safely and proactively experience intimacy with others.

So let's look at how we can help a young person explore the what, how and why questions around intimacy.

Exploring the What

Considering what young people want and need to understand about intimacy
For healthy adolescent development, young people need the chance to explore how to develop friendships built on trust and openness with each other. In their early teens, young people may show interest in developing intimate friendships with their peers, and they might also develop romantic crushes on people they admire and want to be like. They might prefer to hang out in larger, mixed-gender groups where they experience short-lived crushes or relationships. Although we might view this behaviour as chaotic, even problematic, the reality is that this is an important stage for young people in developing their understanding of and skills around negotiating healthy intimacy with others.

Whether online or in person, negotiating intimacy with another person is incredibly difficult. Young people are having to interpret the subtle cues and subtexts that are communicated: 'What does that emoji mean?' 'Why did he send that to her when he says he likes me?' 'Why does she sit on my lap at youth group but only wants to be friends?' For the vast majority, this awakening to their interest in developing intimate relationships coincides with accessing social media. They're more aware than previous generations of the risks of sharing themselves intimately on social media, but they're also conscious that, in their peers' eyes, opting out often isn't an option. One pre-teen told me, 'I half want to be on it [social media] because everyone else is but also I'm worried about making a mistake or seeing everyone else's mistakes.' On the one hand she craved the opportunities for intimacy with her peers that social media would give her, but she feared how vulnerable that might make her. Thinking about the positive ways she could do this really helped her.

More for you to consider

- How might you help young people understand the different types of intimacy, and the impact of one type of intimacy on the others?
- One of the best exercises to do with young people is to help them discover their love language. These describe how individuals best receive love from another person: by hearing words of affirmation, when someone does something for them, through receiving gifts, through spending quality time with someone or by physical

touch.[1] Although young people might not be developing intimate relationships until their late teens or early twenties, awareness of their own love language will help them one day to build stronger relationships.

- What might the young people need to know about the challenges that digital communication can present? Negotiating the sending and receiving 'nudes' culture is a daily ordeal for young people. Chatting about what they could do about this can build their critical skills and confidence to resist pressure and develop practical skills to respond in different situations.
- A good starting point in talking about intimacy is to talk about privacy. We're being intimate with someone when we're sharing something private or personal with them.
- If a young person is interested in developing a relationship with someone significantly older or younger, point out that people of different ages might want different things from a relationship. When might you need to flag this up to your safeguarding lead?

Exploring the How

Helping young people explore ways to value and experience aspects of intimacy
On the whiteboard, I drew an uphill gradient and asked the young people, 'If your goal is to get better at sport, what steps might you need to take to help you get to the top of your game?'

We chatted about fitness, skills, joining a team, and so on. We talked about how building a stronger friendship could be similar. The group identified the different 'steps' of being trustworthy – being kind, having fun together, sharing interests, saying sorry, etc. – as things to get good at in order to help the friendship improve. Then I asked if any of them struggled to do these things, like 'being trustworthy' or 'saying sorry'. Lots of nods, so I flipped over the board and drew a downhill gradient. At the bottom of the 'hill' I wrote 'strong friendship' and marked points along the line with the same words from before (being trustworthy, being kind, having fun together, etc.). I invited the young people to flip their thinking: rather than seeing the stuff they had to 'perfect' so they could move up to a strong friendship, seeing the fears and concerns they could let go of that would enable their friendship to grow in intimacy and strength.

Their responses were brilliant and, as is often the way when people open up about what's real for them, this conversation created an intimate moment among us.

There are friendship skills that we want to help a young person develop, but how might we also help the young people to recognize what holds them back from forming strong friendships? Or they may need help to recognize the range of motives other people have for sharing themselves intimately, in person or online. Do they share this person's motive? Is it a good motive? Or is someone putting pressure on them or coercing them? It's important to help them notice the context of a situation and then to take a pause to think for themselves before jumping into an overshare they may later regret.

More for you to consider

- How might you help the young people to work out whether they are wanting a romantic relationship with someone or feeling pressure from peers, or others, to pair up?
- How could you help the young people identify their own motives for sharing themselves physically or emotionally with others? How could you help them read the context?
- How could you help them appreciate deep, loving connections with other people and explore the impact of connection and closeness. This includes helping them with the skills and confidence to develop close friendships built on openness, sharing and trust.
- For the young people who are in relationships, how could you help them appropriately develop a deeper emotional and spiritual intimacy as well as a physical one? It's good to help them see that every type of intimacy benefits from having positive boundaries.

Exploring the Why

Supporting young people to dig deeper into how intimacy fits into the bigger picture of living with God at the centre of their lives

As we help the young people explore their need for healthy intimacy in their friendships and early romantic relationships, we also want to help them connect with a drive to deepen their relationship with God.

Of all the Gospels, John's is the one that strongly and deliberately depicts the up close and personal connection between the Father, the Son and the Spirit. John paints a picture of the intimacy that he, the 'beloved' disciple, had with Jesus: 'Now there was leaning on Jesus' bosom one of His disciples, whom Jesus loved' (John 13.23, NKJV). John takes great delight in using the word 'bosom'. It's the same word that he uses at the start of his Gospel: 'No one has seen God at any time. The only begotten Son, who is in the bosom of the Father, He has declared *Him*' (John 1.18, NKJV). John is saying that Jesus has this position against the Father's side. He's leaning into him.

This is the image Paul adds to when he speaks of the Spirit interceding with the Father on our behalf, with groans that words cannot fathom (see Romans 8.26). The deepest intimacy any of us will ever know is with God the Father, Son and Holy Spirit. This is why we're not surprised that, when he is asked what's the most important thing, Jesus replies, 'Love the Lord your God with all your heart and with all your soul and with all your mind and with all your strength' (Mark 12.28, NIV). He's encouraging us to pour everything into this relationship with God because this is the relationship we're made for and are held and sustained by. There's a trajectory in our lives of always getting closer to God. This journey of spiritual maturity is about an increasing awareness that we are loved by God, no matter what.

More for you to consider
- Explore with the young people some of the stories in Scripture and church history of people who had a deep intimacy with God. What did this look like? What difference did this make to their lives? It's good to stir up the young people's prophetic imagination of all that's possible as they seek a deeper intimacy with God.
- There are some great techniques to help us deal with our need for affirmation and approval, but nothing deals with it as well as a deepening intimacy with God. How could you help the young people to bring their insecurity and need for affirmation and acceptance to God?

12

The integrity thing

Years ago, a youth worker colleague and I took a bunch of north London teenagers to America to visit a Christian youth movement. The young people stayed in pairs with Christian families. One teenage boy on the project had recently become a Christian, in rather unusual circumstances . . .

Sharp, clever and full of killer questions, André finally agreed one Sunday to go to an evening service at his friend's church. Part way through the evening an older man took to the stage to preach about sexual integrity to the room full of young people. 'Jesus was single, never married, never had sex,' he said, 'but look at the impact his life has had on countless people. Just because you are not having sex, it doesn't mean you aren't worth anything.' He went on to share what following Jesus had meant for his own life and how he had made choices about sex. He was like an old soldier telling tales of battles fought and victories won – and André, experiencing church for the first time, was *utterly* captivated. He looked around the room and thought, 'What do you guys believe if it means you can live a whole life like that?' That night, André chose to follow Jesus.

Later, in Florida, he and eleven other North London teenagers spent two weeks with Christian families. One afternoon, we sat on a beach with a few of the members of the hosting church's youth group and listened to them talk about 'wearing the ring' to keep their parents happy. 'It doesn't mean anything to me,' one girl said. 'I'm still going to sleep with my boyfriend.'

My youth group were incredulous. Why would anyone wear a chastity ring if they weren't prepared to live by those values? Some of them felt angry for the young people, sensing the pressure they felt under to keep their church happy. Others felt angry with them for cheapening a decision that for some in that youth group was genuine. It was a fascinating battle of integrity.

That night, André bought a ring, and he didn't take it off until he got married, years later. As his youth worker, I didn't tell him that following Jesus meant he had to wear a chastity ring. What propelled him to follow Jesus and journey down a path of radical sexual surrender was a sermon on abstinence that gave him a vision of integrity that captivated him.

Integrity is the choice to do what you consider to be the right thing, even when no one is looking, even when there's a more convenient option. Integrity has its own sort of courage – it's not a brash heroism. It's the quiet confidence that comes from being at peace with who you are and how you will act.

The word 'integrity' has a beautiful synergy with *shalom*. It's derived from both the French word *intégrité*, meaning blamelessness, purity, and the Latin word *integer*, meaning wholeness, completeness. It's the sense of being truthful in all your actions and consistent in your character. It's 'you do you' because you increasingly know and are at peace with who that is. It's more than simply being true to yourself – it's being true to the beliefs and ideas you have about yourself. In discipleship terms, it's living in undivided devotion to the One we follow. It's God before Google, before self-interest, before status, before all else. It's not about getting things right all the time, but it's about a hunger to live in such a way as to tell the truth about who you are and whose you are. It's little wonder that, in a world of aggressive individualism, the integrity of a lifetime of sexual faithfulness connected meaningfully with a teenage boy sitting in a church one Sunday night.

As young people grow through adolescence, they develop the attitudes and values that shape their moral character – their sense of what is right and wrong. Part of the journey from childhood to adulthood is transitioning from doing the 'right' thing because you want to please an authority figure (or avoid punishment) to doing the right thing because you believe it to be the right thing, or what it is you know God is asking of you. Over time, attitudes and behaviours that come from a deeper sense of purpose and meaning become integrated into our understanding of who we are, or who we want to be. We forgive because we believe in forgiveness. We give because we are generous. The same is true of our choices about sexual behaviours. We act in accordance with what we believe to be the purpose of our sexuality. As choice-making creatures, young people are able not only to react to biological and social cues, but also to make choices about what they will or won't react to. They are not victims of their own instincts – they have agency.

Many of us have been damaged by a toxic accountability culture that sprung up around a bad theology of holiness. As young people in church, we may have felt scrutinized and shunned for mistakes we made or struggles we had. We may not have 'done' anything, but still felt that we were getting things wrong, that we were sinful. When we did make mistakes, we may have been shamed rather than forgiven. This might make us feel understandably cautious about anything that sounds like a new purity code.

Teaching young people to adhere to a sexual purity code is vastly different from helping them explore and practice sexual integrity. Purity codes focus on whether someone is doing the agreed 'right' thing. Integrity is a personal and steadfast commitment to deeply held beliefs. It's possible for the behaviours of someone in either 'camp' to look similar. André wore a chastity ring because it was a sign of his resistance to all forms of intimate sexual activity with another person outside marriage. It wasn't the purity code that he was buying into; it was a life of sexual integrity for the sake of love – love for God, for himself and for others. Whereas a purity code values the external appearance of something, personal integrity values authenticity and being real about mistakes and shortcomings.

Groups of young people choosing to pursue integrity might look quite messy as they are open with their lives and own their mistakes. But Paul would choose that over the 'dogged religious plod' (1 Thessalonians 4.1) of trying to tick the right boxes. Instead, he urged the first Christians to be obedient to Jesus:

> . . . in a living, spirited dance. You know the guidelines we laid out for you from the Master Jesus. God wants you to live a pure life.
> Keep yourselves from sexual promiscuity.
> Learn to appreciate and give dignity to your body, not abusing it, as is so common among those who know nothing of God.
> (1 Thessalonians 4.3–5)

So let's look at how we can help young people explore the what, how and why questions around their integrity.

Exploring the What

Considering what young people want and need to understand about integrity
Young people are free to make choices. Part of their God-created humanity is their free will, but integrity isn't there from birth – it's something they learn from observing other people's integrity and the behaviours associated with it, such as humility and courage. Helping young people understand what integrity is involves helping them to see it in practice. Who are the role models demonstrating integrity in their relationships?

Young people can often feel powerless in the face of the decisions they need to make. A good place to start in helping them explore integrity is for them to consider what choices they do have power over. We can challenge their victim mentality ('It's not my fault') and build their power mentality ('I'm in charge of my choices') by increasing their sense of accountability. For some young people, victim mentality might be expressed in them seeking to shoulder everyone's responsibility. Help them to see that they can only be responsible and make amends for what they themselves have done, not for what others have done.

As they grow, young people enjoy increasing freedom in how they make their choices, which means they're experiencing more-serious consequences. Seeking wise guidance from people they consider have integrity is a good way for them to build those muscles too. As people they might turn to, our role is help them to articulate what matters to them (their values) and to make their choices with as much information and forethought as the situation allows – as well as how to behave with integrity once they've made a mistake.

More for you to consider

- Think about creating real-life scenarios to use with the young people. Or pose some questions like, 'If a young person has decided to not have sex until they're married, what boundaries could they set to help them stick to that?' or, 'What does someone "getting off" with different people in the youth group, while dating someone else, say about their integrity? How would you feel about them leading worship at a church or youth event? What does your response tell you about your views on sexual integrity?' It's good to help them think about the difference that integrity makes in someone's decisions.

- You could talk them through a basic decision-making process and explore how having a simple process in their mind might help them to make decisions with integrity. Could you create a traffic-light system together where the red light is sexual behaviours (or accompanying behaviours) the young person will avoid (e.g., penetrative sex, fingering, accessing online porn, using drugs, getting drunk), the orange light is sexual behaviours they will limit or delay (e.g., masturbation, reading erotic literature, drinking alcohol) and the green light is sexual behaviours they are happy to engage in (e.g., flirting with and kissing their partner, hanging out with friends, meeting new people safely online or in social groups). This needs the young people to own it, so invite them to suggest which light the different sexual activities would go under. The purpose is to help them articulate, ahead of time, their practices of resistance (what they won't do) and engagement (what they will).

Exploring the How

Helping young people explore ways to practice integrity

Learning integrity takes practice – it doesn't happen overnight. Some of the most significant learning happens as we face the consequences of our mistakes and work out what we would do differently next time. As much as we would love to be the ones who teach a young person how to prac-tise integrity, the best learning comes from opening up opportunities (or drawing their attention to opportunities) when this can happen.

Once, when I was driving along with a few young people in my car (we'd been delivering a sex and relationship programme at a local sec-ondary school), I overheard the lads in the back begin to talk quite openly about how sexy the woman walking along the road was. Moments before, they'd been exemplary peer leaders, showing respect and compassion to the young people in the class we'd been leading. I saw this as a great learn-ing opportunity and pulled the car over. I jumped out, ran back down the road and asked the 'sexy' woman if she would mind coming and meet-ing the lads in my car so that they could get to know her a bit. Amazing-ly, she said yes, so we walked back to my car. Tapping on the window, I gesticulated for the lads on the back seat to come out. They did, sheepish-ly. I introduced her to them and asked her some questions about who she was. I thanked her, and then we all went on our way.

Back in the car, the boys were silent. 'I'm not punishing you,' I explained. 'She was a very attractive woman. But there was a point back there where you stopped appreciating her beauty and started talking about her as an object you could use. Each one of you is a remarkable leader. Incredible young men. I know you can behave with more integrity than you see in the world around you. When you do, you will be giants among men.'

And that's who they have become. Maybe this moment helped that process in some small way – I like to think so. But I know that it's when we encourage young people to do hard things that they grow.

More for you to consider

- Think about how you could help a young person to 'choose your hard'. It's hard to go against the flow, but it's also hard to be swept along with the flow into situations where you feel out of your depth. It's hard to end a relationship that's not right or isn't safe, but it's also hard to stay in a relationship that's not healthy. It's hard to work out what God might want you to do in a situation, but it's also hard to rely on your own perspective. Choices are hard, so choose your hard.
- Think about how peer accountability could help them think through and stick to their decision.
- How will you help them to confidently assert their choices, especially in a hostile environment? One technique is called the 'broken record', where you don't explain your answer but just keep saying 'no', over and over, like a broken record. Or they could write down on their phone or on the back of their hand what they want to say, or what their decision is. That way they 'know their script' and can stick to it.
- It's not only when we make mistakes that we need to face the consequences. Sometimes, doing what we consider to be the right thing can carry consequences we need to face. How might you encourage the young people to stand by their choices and take responsibility for the consequences of those actions?
- How might the young people know that they are becoming people of integrity?

Part 2

Exploring the Why

Supporting young people to dig deeper into how integrity fits into the bigger picture of living with God at the centre of their lives

For young people who are following Jesus, being part of a Christian community that consistently reflects God's vision for their lives helps them to develop an internal sense of how they will live with integrity. As God is faithful and authentic in all his relationships, we're called to be the same. Helping young people develop authentic holy habits may take many years to fully form and live out. This can't happen outside a wider community that sustains this journey.

Here are five practices that mark the sort of vibrant, holy, rebel communities that inspire young people to find God's faithfulness and live with integrity in their sexual choices.

I. Practice of grace (or how we work this stuff out together)

Integrity is a way of being that we develop over time and in communities of people who know what it takes to put God at the centre of their lives. Young people need a community that has endless patience and oceans of grace as they work out how to live with integrity. They need to spend time with other Christians who model the practices of grace: honesty, forgiveness, kindness, compassion, listening well, not judging, personal responsibility and repentance. This creates the sort of safe space where young people can both be challenged and sheltered as they face their mistakes and also find forgiveness and grow in courage to put God at the centre of their lives.

2. Practice of presence (or how we find strength on our knees)

The desire for sexual integrity that honours God doesn't happen outside an encounter with God. Talking is good, but encounter with God is better. A young person exploring how following Jesus shapes their life needs a Christian community that knows how to hold space *for* them and *with* them to encounter something of God's majesty, holiness and awesome love. It's like holding a marshmallow on a stick over a fire. It's not the person holding the stick who transforms the marshmallow – it's the heat of the flames. We need to know how to hold a young person in the fire of God's love – and invite God's Spirit to the work of convicting of sin

164

and strengthening the new life that is unfurling within them. For a post-church generation with a spirituality buried under layers of secularism, consumerism and anxiety, this is what connects.

3. Practice of enthusiastic engagement (or how to say yes, and own it)

The pattern of discipleship is such that young people following Jesus need to follow the example of *others* who are living the way of Jesus. As you think about who supports the youth in your church or youth project, consider people who are demonstrating what it looks like to lean in to be people of peace and integrity in their college, school, workplace or community. Who is saying 'yes' to living life to the full and how are they doing that? Surround the young people with people full of stories of God-adventures. How can you all help the young people know what they will say 'yes' to, and why.

4. Practice of resistance (or how to say no, and own it)

Nothing within wider culture supports a young person's decision to resist sexual activity or to choose to believe something different from the status quo about sex. But rather than being an impossible burden, sexual restraint offers a new freedom. Who is demonstrating the freedom that knowing when to say 'no' brings? Young people who are beginning to try out their 'no' need a community of sage warriors who are not afraid to share how it is for them, and why they keep choosing God's way for their sex lives.

5. Practice of shining (or how to witness well)

As it's not easy to say *yes* to Jesus in today's world, a young person is automatically standing out in a way that will draw a lot of curiosity as well as a lot of fire. This is no bad thing as it's par for the course for saints throughout the ages. In choosing to live with sexual integrity, though, they need to know they are not alone. They are part of the diverse and huge body of Christ, and their witness adds to a timeless blaze that inspires others to search for God.

Above all, imagine how you could create around the young people a community that seeks to support and nurture them as they explore putting God at the centre of their lives and choices. Going against the flow isn't easy, so they need cheerleaders and brothers and sisters in arms who will champion them. Why not use these words to speak a blessing over them?

A blessing

We bless you with the freedom to grow and flourish as you journey through adolescence.

We bless you with the confidence to grow in both sexual awareness and a sense of accompanying responsibility.

We bless your curiosity about sex – may you seek the wisdom you need from positive people and places.

We ask that you will be protected from internalizing the lies that your body is bad and your sexual responses are sinful.

We long for you to be resilient in the face of the shame that would drive you away from seeking support from those who want to see you flourish in your God-given potential.

We bless you with watchful assertiveness over those who would try to drag you into false sexual habits, damaging beliefs and destructive sexual behaviours.

We bless you with discernment over the patterns of thought and behaviour that develop out of sexual exploration of your body.

We bless your courage as you seek to make God the centre of your life.

We bless your hunger for the sweetness of adventure and for the wonder of love.

May God be with you, as you work yourself out and work his wisdom in.

May God strengthen you, as you resist damaging behaviours and speak out for others.

May God restore you, as you face your regrets and own your mistakes.

May God redeem you, as you reimagine the choices you will make in embracing God's vision for your whole life.

May God empower you, as you follow the way of Jesus.

May you never lose the fire, the fun, the possibility or the brilliance of being you.

13

The thing is

I once heard an astronaut talk about being on a space station when COVID-19 broke out on Earth. Looking down from the dark void of space, she couldn't get her head around the fact that 7.5 billion people were all being affected by the same virus. She felt so far away, so helpless in the face of such distress. I wonder how many of us might feel the same when we look at the young people in our church or youth group?

Culture is moving rapidly. There may be things our young people are facing that we never had to think about. We can all sense that overwhelming fear of, 'What happens if I say the wrong thing?' and the enemy would *love* to sow the seed of doubt into your ability to connect well with young people. And yet, if somehow this book has made out that having conversations with young people about sex is complicated, then I apologize. Seasons change and cultures shift, but I've yet to meet a young person who isn't won over by a cup of tea with three sugars and a chance to be truly listened to. (By the way, this isn't factual. Always check how many sugars a teenager might want!) Conversations with young people are not complicated. But they are important. And if a conversation with you means they'll experience something deeper of God's *shalom*, I hope this book will help us be ready for them.

Proximity

The Apostle Paul is a great role model for anyone who ministers to young people. We know from his missionary journeys, recorded in the book of Acts, that he and his close friends would often stay for up to three years with a new Christian community they helped to plant. They put down roots. They did life with these young believers, allowing those they taught to see up close and personal what living a God-centred, Jesus-surrendered life looks like.

Paul was a rabbi who walked with his disciples, prioritizing character over programmes. At one point, he referred to himself (the most powerful man in the early church) as a mother: 'We were gentle among you, like a nurse tenderly caring for her own children. So deeply do we care for you that we are determined to share with you not only the gospel of God but also our own selves' (1 Thessalonians 2.7–8, NRSV). His purpose in walking closely with them was nothing less than the renewal of *all* things, because he knew that a life transformed by encounter with the Spirit of Jesus is a life that can transform the world. So he prayed:

> May the Master pour on the love so it fills your lives and splashes over on everyone around you . . . May you be infused with strength and purity, filled with confidence in the presence of God our Father when our Master Jesus arrives with all his followers.
> (1 Thessalonians 3.11–13)

If there's one thing I've learnt – and am still learning – when it comes to talking to young people about sex, it is that our passion and proximity are so much more important than our perfection.

In many ways, this book feels like it's been a lifetime in the making. As I've written these pages, I've recalled the faces of young people I've known over the years. I can remember conversations with some of them in minute detail. Sitting in a chapel cave on a beach in Devon with young people as we discussed celibacy. Waiting in a layby on the way to a youth festival with a youth group and a broken-down minibus, chatting about whether oral sex is sex. Holding a young person's hand as we waited for the results of her pregnancy test. Sitting in church with a teenage boy who was sobbing his heart out after just 'coming out' to his parents. Powerful memories of extraordinary young people. They've been in my heart as I've been writing. Even as I write these last sentences, I've just received a text from one of them: 'Me and this guy are not dating any more.'

Woah, I think. *What's the backstory to that? No emojis. No more information. Is she OK?* My mind goes to all the scenarios that might have led to this.

'How are you feeling about that?' I text back.

'Honestly, completely fine,' she replies.

I pause – 'fine' is a tough word to translate – so I do a bit of digging. 'Does it feel like the right thing that it's over?'

'Yes.'

Gosh, I hate mobile phones right now. What does 'yes' mean? 'OK, then.' I type back. 'How is the "forcing my dogs to take their medicine" thing going?'

Lots of emojis, followed by, 'Terrible. Having to hide it in ham. Me and Tim have agreed to stay friends.'

'The ham is a genius move,' I reassure her. 'And I'm glad you and Tim want to stay friends. If you want to chat about that, let's do it!'

What she says next encapsulates everything this book is about. 'Oh man, I've been dying to chat with you about that. Can I come and see you Monday?'

It's a reminder that the best chats are the ones that happen when they're needed, and that the biggest privilege is being someone a young person finds easy to turn to when they need those chats to happen. Information, stats, ideas, pithy phrases and funny illustrations are all good, but, in the end, what makes the difference in the young people's lives is having *you* in their corner, ready to listen, full of compassion, armed with wisdom and a whole lot of faith in them. But isn't it frustrating how we often forget this and think we need to be the experts who are never lost for words or overwhelmed by the world our young people are growing up in? What's more, we can sometimes forget that the Holy Spirit is in these conversations too – something I was reminded of as I walked around a reservoir with a young person I know.

Make it your thing

As we were walking, the sun began to set and flocks of small gulls flew over our heads and settled on the water. Discarded shopping trolleys and the odd trainer littered the ground, but somehow these little birds managed to give this place an air of wonder. We watched them for a while.

'They're my favourite bird,' Kelly said. 'Well, my favourite all-time animal, actually.'

We were silent for a while. As far as I'm concerned, gulls are rats with wings. I feel the same way about pigeons. Years of living in London does that to you.

'Why do you love them so much?' I asked.

'Look at them,' she replied. 'They're really small. Nothing else is here. It's not exactly pretty here. But the seagulls don't care.'

I was so moved by Kelly's capacity to see something wondrous in the mundane that, when I got home, I googled seagulls. They're pretty cool creatures. Known for being fearless, seagulls are intrepid explorers and able to travel great distances. Being noisy birds, they can make themselves heard over the din of city traffic and other wildlife. This felt like a prompt, a prayer for us as leaders, carers and parents, that we would have courage to disciple young people well.

But it's also a prayer for our young people – that they would be fearless in exploring their one, wild life, eager to launch out into the adventure of following Jesus, whatever the cost. That, above all the noise of culture, fear and confusion, they would tune their lives into the One who is the power and the wisdom of God. That they would know they are loved, lift up their heads and make their voice heard.

> Never walk away from Wisdom – she guards your life;
> love her – she keeps her eye on you.
> Above all and before all, do this: Get Wisdom!
> Write this at the top of your list: Get Understanding!
> Throw your arms around her – believe me, you won't regret it;
> never let her go – she'll make your life glorious.
> She'll garland your life with grace,
> she'll festoon your days with beauty.
> (Proverbs 4.6–9)

It may be that God, in his infinite wisdom, has been speaking to you through this book too. So what's your hope, your prayer for the young people you know who are facing the challenges of growing up in life and faith in today's world? Your hope for them is big. Audacious, even. Even if it's simple. Freedom. Safety. Wholeness. *Shalom*. Ask yourself what it might require of you not only to pray this prayer, but also to walk with this young person into this truth. What might it look like for you to re-imagine conversations with them about sex, or anything they want to talk about?

Now, it's over to you. Because there are young people who need us. They need us to talk. They need us to listen. And they need us to be willing to talk, not about a 'thing' or an 'it.' No, they need us to talk about SEX. So let's start talking.

Rachel x

Part 3

All in all, the idea of sex – although on one hand deeply desired –
absolutely terrifies me because it has been built up to be such a
huge thing. I don't know whether this is solely the church's fault or
whether the sex-obsessed culture we live in plays an equal role, but
I feel ultimately damaged by it all.
Young person, A Christian Youth Sex Survey

I think the churches I am involved in portray a positive view of sex
and that young people feel it gives them confidence to explore their
thoughts and what they think Jesus is asking of them.
Youth leader, The Big Sex Chat

Appendix 1

A Christian Youth Sex Survey: a survey of Christian young people aged 16–21, 2020

551 participants

Q1. This survey is for 16–25-year-olds living in the UK who self-identify as Christians or are part of a church. Is this you?
Answered: 551; Skipped: 0

Yes	89.84%
No	10.16%

Q2. So just before we get started, I'd love to get to hear a bit more about you if that's OK. First, what gender do you identify with?
Answered: 551; Skipped: 0

Male	31.58%
Female	66.97%
Prefer not to say	0.73%
Other	0.73%

Q3. Where are you currently living?
Answered: 549; Skipped: 2

Scotland	4.55% (25 young people)
Northern Ireland	3.28% (18 young people)
Wales	1.09% (6 young people)
North East	2.55% (14 young people)
North West	10.2% (56 young people)
Yorkshire and Humber	4.74% (26 young people)
West Midlands	9.11% (50 young people)

East Midlands	11.66% (64 young people)
South West	12.2% (67 young people)
South East	21.13% (116 young people)
East of England	8.56% (47 young people)
Greater London	10.93% (60 young people)

Q4. What church denomination do you consider yourself to be part of?
Answered: 549; Skipped: 2

Church of England	43.17% (237 young people)
Catholic	1.09% (6 young people)
Baptist	14.75% (81 young people)
URC	0.36% (2 young people)
Methodist	3.28% (18 young people)
Free Methodist	0.73% (4 young people)
Pentecostal	6.01% (33 young people)
Independent	9.29% (51 young people)
New Frontiers	3.10% (17 young people)
Brethren	0% (0 young people)
Other (please specify)	18.21% (100 young people)

Q5. In churches you have been part of, which of the following messages about sex do you think have been communicated to you? [tick as many as you want]
Answered: 551; Skipped: 0

God thinks it's OK to have sex before marriage	5.63% (31 young people)
Other (please specify)	12.16% (67 young people)
Nothing has been communicated	14.7% (81 young people)
God thinks sex is only for straight people	45.37% (250 young people)
God thinks sex is good	57.35% (316 young people)
God is disappointed if Christians have sex outside marriage	65.15% (359 young people)

Q6. Do you think your church should teach Christian young people about sex?
Answered: 551; Skipped: 0

| Yes | 93.65% (516 young people) |

No	3.27% (18 young people)
Don't know	3.09% (17 young people)

Q7. Do you think your church should be teaching Christian young people that they shouldn't have sex before they're married?
Answered: 550; Skipped: 1

Yes	48% (264 young people)
No	31.27% (172 young people)
Don't know	20.73% (114 young people)

Q8. Do you think your church should be teaching Christian young people that sex is between one man and one woman?
Answered: 547; Skipped: 4

Yes	41.13% (225 young people)
No	46.98% (257 young people)
Don't know	11.88% (65 young people)

Q9. Do you agree with what your church teaches about sex?
Answered: 551; Skipped: 0

Yes	37.93% (209 young people)
No	22.5% (124 young people)
Don't know	39.56% (218 young people)

Q10. When it comes to your choices about sex, who do you look to for advice and support? [tick your top 3]
Answered: 549; Skipped: 2

My friends	64.48% (354 young people)
I google it / do my own research	38.43% (211 young people)
I pray about it	35.7% (196 young people)
Christian teachers / speakers I trust	32.06% (176 young people)
I study Scripture	30.6% (168 young people)
My parents or other family members	27.14% (149 young people)
Church youth leader or someone from the youth team	24.23% (133 young people)
I don't tend to ask anyone	23.32% (128 young people)
Other members of the church I attend	13.84% (76 young people)

My church leader   13.3% (73 young people)
Opinions of YouTubers, social media personalities,
celebrities, etc.   11.66% (64 young people)
Don't know   4.37% (24 young people)
Teacher at school or college   4.19% (23 young people)
Parents of my friends   2.55% (14 young people)

Q11. If you think your church should be talking with Christian young people about sex, what topics would you like them to talk about? [choose your top 5]

Answered: 546; Skipped: 5

How to have healthy relationships   82.78% (452 young people)
What the Bible teaches about sex   63.92% (349 young people)
Setting sexual boundaries in premarital
relationships   60.07% (328 young people)
Dealing with feelings of guilt and shame   59.89% (327 young people)
Sexual consent   54.58% (298 young people)
Masturbation   51.83% (283 young people)
The impact of online porn   50.73% (277 young people)
Emotional and physical safety   47.25% (258 young people)
Acceptance of LGBTQI+ relationships   45.6% (249 young people)
Inclusion of LGBTQI+ people   45.42% (248 young people)
What the Bible teaches about going out with
someone who isn't a Christian   41.58% (227 young people)
Handling peer pressure   39.01% (213 young people)
Sexual violence   32.23% (176 young people)
Dating apps and other sexual technologies
(sex-capable AI, super connected
sex toys, etc.)   27.66% (151 young people)

Q12. What do you think is the MOST IMPORTANT THING churches can do to help Christian young people in this area?

Answered: 514; Skipped: 37

Sample of responses:

- Teach young people how to be safe and create a supportive environment.
- Be open for communication rather than putting up barriers and taboo – it's so dangerous when an institution like the Church starts cutting communication about such important things.
- Be accepting and supportive without being judging or condemning, regardless of the situation or circumstances. Help them to see their true worth and value.
- Teach with integrity.
- Discuss it. And stay strong with what the Bible says is right in the eyes of God.
- Be open and accepting of what the youth speak about; don't belittle them or make them feel ashamed for what they have or haven't done. Just be welcoming for them and allow them to speak without the feeling of judgement.
- Not teach people from a place of inducing shame; teach them God's design for sex and why he created it that way – the beauty in it. But get rid of the whole 'it's like handing your husband a dirty glass of water' rhetoric.
- Be open, accepting and start the conversation.
- Contraceptive and sexual abuse support.
- To emphasize that sexual sin is the same as all sins: God doesn't like them. But that there shouldn't be shame, and to account for the fact that some Christians will have had sex but it's about how they decide to continue living.
- Be loving and accepting of church youth as they learn about sex and make up their own opinions on it.
- Create a safe space to listen and learn, not just to give out the same advice to every situation.
- Hmm, anonymous forums, as youth tend to not like the subject when people know who asked the question(s).
- More education without judgement and complete transparency between the church and the young people. Potentially focus more on female experiences of masturbation because it is never spoken about. It is only mentioned to the boys.

- Talk about it more and not make it something that isn't spoken about. If we can discuss these topics it would be so much easier to understand people's opinions and what the right choices to make are.
- To not make young Christian people feel ashamed or embarrassed about their sex life.
- To provide a safe space, where we just talk about what we think with others our age, free of judgement, and to ask non-Christian questions about sex.
- Build their confidence and tell them it's not a frightening thing! Also make them aware of sexual abuse and violence, and that they do have a voice and can say no.
- Explain different options/ways of thinking and explain WHY people think that/the rationale behind it. I think we need to be able to make informed choices, but also to live our own lives.
- Having someone they can turn to and talk about it without it being weird.

Appendix 2

The Big Sex Chat: a survey of youth leaders, 2020

318 participants

Q1. In churches you have been part of, which of the following messages about sex do you think have been communicated to young people?
Answered: 317; Skipped: 1

Other (please specify)	8.52% (27 youth leaders)
Sex is dirty and sexual feelings are dangerous	9.15% (29 youth leaders)
Nothing – churches don't want to talk about sex	31.23% (99 youth leaders)
Sex is only for heterosexual marriage	53.31% (169 youth leaders)
God created sex and gave us boundaries for our safety and success	59.62% (189 youth leaders)
Having sex before marriage / outside of marriage is wrong and will have damaging consequences	60.25% (191 youth leaders)

Q2. What is the impact of the way this church/these churches relate to young people about sex?
Answered: 282; Skipped: 36
The 282 responses fall into either Positive, Negative or Mixed/Neutral/Unknown.

We identified keywords about the principal themes. Keywords like Bible, purity, healthy, shame, etc. Each keyword is an attempt to sum up a variety of related ideas. For example, the shorthand keyword 'safe space' is taken to mean a culture of free, honest, non-judgemental and open conversations. 'Purity' is used to cover any time the response talked about purity, dirtiness or similar contamination-framed replies.

This categorizing of the data suggests that 22 per cent of respondents believe their church's approach to teaching young people about sex has a positive impact, 57% a negative impact and 21% it's either mixed, neutral or unknown.

Positive 22%
Negative 57%
Neutral 21%

Looking at the frequency of categories as a total and separating them by trends of positive and negative, we are able to identify the following most common categories;

Shame 30% – these comments suggest the approach increases a sense of shame in young people.
Estranging 23% – these comments suggest the approach drives young people away from the church or creates distance between young people and God.
Silence 22% – these comments suggest the approach is about not talking to young people about sex.
Damaging 17% – these comments suggest the approach is actively damaging to young people.
Safe spaces 15% – these comments suggest the approach offers young people a space to think, reflect and make positive decisions.
A sample of responses demonstrating a range of views:

> I think it results in people fearing sex and fearing people who are comfortable in their sexuality. For those who have not or do not conform to the heteronormative/marital ideals that the church upholds for sexual relationships, it results in guilt and shame and self-loathing. The grey area and lack of friendly and informal discussions about sex in a church setting results in broken-down or uneasy Christian friendships that lack honesty and, sometimes, respect for the other's choices. I think that this eventually becomes a huge reason people leave the church and an excuse for people avoiding church. I think

that there is a lack of counselling and discussion for those who are in heterosexual marriages, and even less (often none) space for discussion for those unmarried or members of the LGBT community.

Sometimes, if it's not handled correctly, it can make it a taboo subject that young people don't want to talk about or are ashamed of, instead of there being an honest and non-judgemental space for vulnerability in struggles, accountability, prayer, repentance and exhortation from Scripture.

It helps them see that the church is willing to engage, discuss and help. That although the Bible holds us to very clear guidelines for sex, there are reasons for those guidelines that are for our benefit.

I don't think they do relate. In my experience it becomes alienating for young people within a church environment as they are in the midst of trying to figure out these big life questions in the current climate of sexual freedom as well as the big conversations around sexuality.

There's probably too much of a focus on the 'sin' and less on the 'gift'. For young people who are experimenting, it can leave them feeling that they have failed once and for all and there's no going back to being a virgin. We don't talk about other sin in the same way so we need more of a focus on being made whole and right before God – as we would do with other type of sin. The unwrapped, messed-up present analogy has to go!

Shame. So much shame. And this leads to a lack of honesty in our conversations. Not just in how young people talk to leaders, but also to each other, and when young people don't have safe spaces to talk about this stuff, they're left incredibly vulnerable and even unsafe.

Q3. If you were trying to describe how the UK Church's engagement with young people in this area has changed over the last ten years, what would you identify as the key shifts?
Answered: 315; Skipped: 3

It's not really changed	15.87% (50 youth leaders)
Other (please specify)	15.87% (50 youth leaders)
Churches are more aware of young people's sexual development so they are more responsive to their needs and supportive of their journey and beliefs	22.86% (72 youth leaders)
Churches are more likely to pull back from this conversation for fear of getting it wrong or hurting young people	28.57% (90 youth leaders)
Churches see their job as holding on to traditional views on sex and relationships	39.68% (125 youth leaders)
Churches are realizing the need for more open conversations and pastoral support in this area	53.97% (170 youth leaders)

Q4. When does the topic of sex come up in your work with young people?

Answered: 314; Skipped: 4

Other (please specify)	9.87% (31 youth leaders)
It doesn't	13.06% (41 youth leaders)
It's part of the core curriculum of the work with young people	36.94% (116 youth leaders)
When we ask young people what they want to discuss	39.81% (125 youth leaders)
If there's a situation affecting the young people that needs addressing either individually or as a group	44.9% (141 youth leaders)
When they raise it in one-to-one mentoring / pastoral conversations	45.86% (144 youth leaders)

Q5. How often have you initiated conversations with young people about sex in the last year?

Answered: 316; Skipped: 2

Frequently	4.43% (14 youth leaders)
Fairly often	11.71% (37 youth leaders)
Never	16.14% (51 youth leaders)
Very rarely	33.86% (107 youth leaders)

| Sometimes | 33.86% (107 youth leaders) |

Q6. What are the barriers to initiating these conversations with young people?

Answered: 309; Skipped: 9

Other (please specify)	39.48% (122 youth leaders)
The young people aren't asking questions about sex so it doesn't feel appropriate for me to raise it	38.51% (119 youth leaders)
I don't know what my church believes or would want me to say. Until it articulates its approach, I don't feel able to open up conversation with the youth on this topic	22.65% (70 youth leaders)
I don't know what I'd say and would prefer to say nothing rather than cause confusion or damage	11.65% (36 youth leaders)
I don't know	6.15% (19 youth leaders)
I don't see it as part of my role	3.24% (10 youth leaders)

Q7. What would motivate you to have these conversations with young people?

Answered: 315; Skipped: 3

I don't want young people to feel full of shame and confusion with no one or nowhere safe to ask their questions	79.05% (249 youth leaders)
My role is about helping young people in all areas of their life, including relationships, sex and sexuality	60.95% (192 youth leaders)
I want them to know the truth as taught in Scripture so that they can make the right choices and protect themselves from regret, and hurting themselves and others	50.79% (160 youth leaders)
I think it's important for young people to understand their church's or Christianity's teaching about sex, sexuality and relationships	44.76% (141 youth leaders)

I wish someone had talked to me about
these things when I was a teenager   36.19% (114 youth leaders)
Other (please specify)   6.98% (22 youth leaders)

Q8. Which of the following topics are most important to cover when talking to young people about sex? Please choose your top five (this can be over time, not just in one chat!)

Answered: 315; Skipped: 3

Physical and emotional safety	67.3% (212 youth leaders)
Consent	65.4% (206 youth leaders)
Digital technology (online porn, dating apps, etc.)	56.83% (179 youth leaders)
Choices, personal responsibility and consequences	55.24% (174 youth leaders)
Marriage, exclusivity and commitment	48.25% (152 youth leaders)
Identity	45.71% (144 youth leaders)
Peer pressure	41.9% (132 youth leaders)
LGBTQAI +	40% (126 youth leaders)
Intimacy	34.92% (110 youth leaders)
Handling regret and shame	33.33% (105 youth leaders)
Power, coercion and abuse	30.16% (95 youth leaders)
Communication skills	22.86% (72 youth leaders)
Moral integrity	21.27% (67 youth leaders)
Sexual purity	17.78% (56 youth leaders)
Other (please specify)	7.94% (25 youth leaders)
Justice	6.67% (21 youth leaders)

Q9. What has been most helpful in shaping your response to young people on the topic of sex?

Answered: 318; Skipped: 0

My own reading of scripture	13.21% (42 youth leaders)
Christian teaching, books and talks on the subject	25.47% (81 youth leaders)
Training, teaching and resources from outside the Christian community	11.01% (35 youth leaders)
My own life experience	32.7% (104 youth leaders)

My experience of working with
young people   17.61% (56 youth leaders)

Q10. Which of the following would help you feel more equipped to engage young people in conversations about sex?
Answered: 316; Skipped: 2
More practical training and evidence-based
resources to use with young people   42.72% (135 youth leaders)
An opportunity for deeper theological
teaching and engagement to help me
understand what I believe   18.35% (58 youth leaders)
A clear idea of what issues young people
struggle with   17.72% (56 youth leaders)
The support of my line manager / church
leadership / parents of the young people, etc. 12.66% (40 youth leaders)
Other (please specify)   5.7% (18 youth leaders)
A chance to reflect more on my own story and
how I relate to these topics   2.85% (9 youth leaders)

Appendix 3
Extra resources

Youthscape provides diverse resources supporting youth work across the UK. Its national training courses cater to both professionals and youth workers, currently covering issues like self-harm, anxiety and emotional well-being. Its church-related services, such as Launchpad, Youth Work Sunday and Youthwork Essentials, support churches to get youth ministry going and growing. It offers different kinds of academic study, from annual lectures to accredited qualifications in youth work and theology. Youthscape's Centre for Research is dedicated to studying the ever-shifting landscape of youth culture and its innovation team creates resources to equip youth leaders to best serve young people today.
https://www.youthscape.co.uk

Urban Saints runs seminars for all parents, teachers, church leaders, youth and children's leaders, and anyone who cares about children and young people with special / additional needs or disabilities.
https://www.urbansaints.org/allinclusive

ACET UK provides faith-based training for school relationships and sex education (RSE) in the UK. Its highly regarded Esteem RSE training course encompasses both training to enable people to become relationships and sexual health educators and direct provision of RSE sessions in secondary schools, alternative youth provision and other youth settings. With RSE gaining statutory status in all secondary schools, it can give you what you need to be an effective, confident and wise educator for young people and help you to stay up to date with the new government policy guidelines.
https://www.acet-uk.com/esteem

The Center for Faith, Sexuality & Gender is a collaboration of Christian pastors, leaders and theologians who aspire to be the Church's most trusted source of theological and practical guidance on questions related to sexuality and gender. It offers small-group material, educational videos, podcasts, blogs, youth curriculum and other resources.
http://www.centerforfaith.com

Diverse Church provides pastoral care to support and encourage LGBT+ Christians to grow in their faith. Its online communities provide a safe space for LGBT+ Christians to share their experience of their sexuality, to discuss the interrelation of their sexuality and Christian theology, and to support each other through prayer and encouragement.
https://diversechurch.website

Further reading

10 Questions Every Teen Should Ask (and Answer) about Christianity
Rebecca McLaughlin
(Wheaton, Il: Crossway, 2021)
In this helpful book – written both for Christian teens and for those who think Jesus is just a fairy tale character – Rebecca McLaughlin invites readers aged twelve to fifteen to dig deep into hard questions for themselves and perhaps discover that the things that once looked like roadblocks to faith might actually be signposts.

The Man You're Made to Be: A book about growing up
Martin Saunders
(London: SPCK, 2019)
This brilliant book offers teenage boys a framework for navigating life as a Christian, and not only suggests where healthy boundaries might lie but also invites them to see faith in Christ as the most exciting, purpose-finding and potential-releasing adventure imaginable.

Purposeful Sexuality: A short Christian introduction
Ed Shaw
(London: IVP, 2021)
This book explores the Bible's deepest answers to this question in ways that will help everyone to appreciate and enjoy God's purposeful gift of sexuality – whatever your past history, current situation or sexual orientation might be.

Acknowledgements

Many wonderful people have inspired and sustained me as I've written this book.

I want to thank Elizabeth Neep for being a brilliantly encouraging and insightful editor, and for having the same surname as my three-year-old's favourite TV character!

I'm indebted to fantastic friends who were so generous with their wisdom, support and expertise, especially Martin Saunders, Dr Lucie Shuker, Luke Aylen, Gareth Cheeseman, Jason Royce and Sarah Percival Long.

Thank you to the glorious young people at Minster Youth who have kept me rooted, laughing and inspired to love Jesus and eat more toast.

I'm grateful to the young people and youth leaders who took part in online surveys, round-table discussions or phone interviews with me. Each story, comment and conversation has played a significant role in shaping some of the ideas in the book, so thank you for trusting me.

Finally, thank you to Jason – baker of the best cookies, builder of the biggest fires and architect of the wildest adventures. And to Daisy and Thomas – you fill my world with dens and slime and make me feel like the richest person on earth.

Notes

I The purity hangover

1 Linda Kay Klein, *Pure: Inside the evangelical movement that shamed a generation of young women and how I broke free* (New York: Touchstone, 2018), cited in Stephanie Dubick, 'How Evangelical Purity Culture Can Lead to a Lifetime of Sexual Shame' *Vice*, 16 October 2018 (available online at: <https://www.vice.com/en/article/pa98x8/purity-culture-linday-kay-klein-pure-review>, accessed June 2021).

2 Donna-Marie Cooper, 'Was Tertullian a Misogynist? A re-examination of this charge based on a rhetorical analysis of Tertullian's work', thesis for the degree of Doctor of Philosophy in Theology, University of Exeter, September 2012, p. 4 (available online at: <https://ore. exeter.ac.uk/repository/bitstream/handle/10871/10124/CooperD. pdf?sequence=2>, accessed June 2021).

3 With thanks to Gareth Cheeseman for helping me collate and understand these findings.

4 Lauren Winner, *Real Sex: The naked truth about chastity* (Grand Rapids: Brazos Press, 2005), cited in Kate Harris, 'Book Review – Real Sex: the naked truth about chastity', Covenant Eyes, 20 August 2009 (available online at: <https://www.covenanteyes.com/2009/08/20/book-review-real-sex-the-naked-truth-about-chastity/>, accessed June 2021).

5 Jeff Diamant, 'Half of U.S. Christians say casual sex between consenting adults is sometimes or always acceptable', Pew Research Centre, 31 August 2020 (available online at: <https://www.pewresearch.org/fact-tank/2020/08/31/half-of-u-s-christians-say-casual-sex-between-consenting-adults-is-sometimes-or-always-acceptable/>, accessed May 2021).

6 Nick Shepherd, *Faith Generation: Retaining young people and growing the Church* (London: SPCK, 2016).

7 N. T. Wright, *Paul For Everyone: The prison letters* (London: SPCK, 2002), p. 59.

2 Rising strong

1 Dr Saul McLeod, 'Erik Erikson's Stages of Psychosocial Development', Simply Psychology, 2018 (available online at: <https://www.simplypsychology.org/Erik-Erikson.html>, accessed June 2021).

2 Carolyn Steber, 'How To Be More Comfortable With Yourself', Bustle, 16 December 2015 (available online at: <https://www.bustle.com/articles/130190-6-ways-to-be-more-comfortable-with-yourself>, accessed May 2021).

3 Cited in Jayce Long, 'The Relationship between Identity Formation and Faith Maturity', Florida State University College of Human Sciences, spring 2012, p. 31 (available online at: <https://www.semanticscholar.org/paper/The-relationship-between-identity-formation-and-Long/c52992017c651ff0ddc8e63521f21c84f4e6acf9>, accessed May 2021).

4 'What are the Stages of Faith?', CAINA (available online at <https://cainaweb.org/stages-of-faith/>, accessed June 2021).

5 Jayce Long, 'The Relationship between Identity Formation and Faith Maturity', p. 32.

6 Lewis Corner, 'Reclaiming the word "queer": what does it mean in 2019?', *Gay Times*, 2019 (available online at: <https://www.gaytimes.co.uk/life/reclaiming-the-word-queer-what-does-it-mean-in-2019/>, accessed May 2021).

7 Cited in Corner, 'Reclaiming the word "queer"'.

8 Rebecca Nicholson, '"I'm a bisexual homoromantic": why young Brits are rejecting old labels', *The Guardian*, 18 August 2015 (available online at: <https://www.theguardian.com/society/2015/aug/18/bisexual-british-adults-define-gay-straight-heterosexual>, accessed May 2021).

9 SciencexMedia at Global Development, 'Lisa Diamond – How Different are Female and Male Sexual Orientation?' YouTube, 17 October 2013 (available online at: <https://www.youtube.com/watch?v=C1wa1kYQAJQ&ab_channel=SciencexMediaatGlobalDevelopment>, accessed May 2021).

10 Interview with Luke Aylen, priest and writer.

11 Mental health First Aid Course HandBook (London: Mental Health First Aid England), p. 13.

12 Preston M. Sprinkle, *Embodied: Transgender identities, the Church, and what the Bible has to say* (Colorado Springs: David C. Cook, 2021), pp. 55–6.

13 Paul J. Wright, 'A longitudinal analysis of us adults' pornography exposure: Sexual socialization, selective exposure, and the moderating role of unhappiness.', *Journal of Media Psychology: Theories, Methods, and Applications*, 24(2), 67–76 (available online at: <https://psycnet.apa.org/record/2012-24262-003>, accessed June 2021).

14 G. M. Hald, N. M. Malamuth and C. Yuen, 'Pornography and Attitudes Supporting Violence Against Women: Revisiting the Relationship in Nonexperimental Studies', Aggression and Behavior 36(1), 14–20 (2010) (available online at: <doi:10.1002/ab.20328>, accessed June 2021); M. Allen, T. Emmers, L. Gebhardt and M. A. Giery, 'Exposure to Pornography and Acceptance of the Rape Myth' *Journal of Communication*, 45(1), 5–26 (1995).

3 Yes, no, maybe

1 'Pure Novelty Spurs the Brain', *Science Daily*, 27 August 2006 (available online at: <https://www.sciencedaily.com/releases/2006/08/060826180547.htm>, accessed June 2021).

2 Jenny Taylor, *A Wild Constraint: The case for chasity* (London: Continuum, 2008), p. 69.

4 Pubes, nudes and dudes

1 'The Stages of Puberty: Development in Girls and Boys', Healthline, 23 August 2018 (available online at: <https://www.healthline.com/health/parenting/stages-of-puberty#tanner-stage-3>, accessed May 2021).

2 'Top Ten Facts About Period Poverty in the U.K.', The Borgen Project, 15 July 2019 (available online at: https://borgenproject.org/top-10-facts-about-period-poverty-in-the-uk/>, accessed May 2021).

3 'Girls Fear Criticism for Being Themselves', Girlguiding, 7 August 2020 (available online at: <https://www.girlguiding.org.uk/what-we-do/our-stories-and-news/news/girls--fear-criticism-for-being-themselves/>, accessed June 2021).

4 'State of the Nation 2019: Children and Young People's Wellbeing', Department for Education, October 2019, p. 47 (available online at: <https://assets.publishing.service.gov.uk/government/uploads/system/ uploads/attachment_data/file/906693/State_of_the_Nation_2019_ young_people_children_wellbeing.pdf>, accessed June 2021).

5 Michael S. Patton, 'Twentieth-Century Attitudes Toward Masturbation', in *Journal of Religion and Heath*, Vol 25, No 4 (1986), p. 299.

6 Roger F. Hurding, *Understanding Adolescence (Christian Doctor Series)* (London: Hodder & Stoughton, 1989), p. 109.

7 Major Charlie Curreri, 'Pornography – Intimacy without Cost', in *Carer and Counsellor*, Vol 8, No 1, 1, p. 9.

8 David G. Benner (ed.), *Baker Encyclopedia of Psychology* (Grand Rapids: Baker Book House, 1985), p. 687.

5 The Disney gospel

1 'Moralistic Therapeutic Deism' is a term widely used in youth ministry, originally coined by Christian Smith and Melina Lundquist Denton (original source unknown).

2 Quoted in Jonathan M. Lunde, 'A Summons to Covenantal Discipleship', C. S. Lewis Institute, summer 2011 (available online at: <https://www.cslewisinstitute.org/Summons_to_Covenantal_ Discipleship_Lunde_Single-Page_Full_Article>, accessed June 2021).

3 Tim Keller, *Center Church: Doing balanced, gospel-centered ministry in your city* (Grand Rapids: Zondervan, 2012), p. 31.

4 Dietrich Bonhoeffer, *The Cost of Discipleship* (Simon and Shuster reprint, 1995), pp. 45–9.

5 Attributed to Preston Sprinkle.

6 N. T. Wright, *Paul For Everyone, Romans Part 2: Chapters 9–16* (London: SPCK, 2009), p. 40.

7 David Kinnaman, Goodreads (available online at: <https:// www.goodreads.com/author/quotes/524557.David_ Kinnaman#:~:text=%E2%80%9CWhen%20Millennials%20 face%20turmoil%2C%20they,God%2C%20they%20need%20 God.%E2%80%9D&text=%E2%80%9CMany%20outsiders%20cla- rified%20that%20they,our%20methods%20and%20our%20attitudes>, accessed June 2021).

6 Rebel community

1 Rachel McLaughlin, *Confronting Christianity: 12 hard questions for the world's largest religion* (Wheaton: Crossway, 2019), p. 133.

2 'Suzerain Treaties & The Covernant Documents in the Bible', Notes from lectures of Dr. Meredith Kline (available online at: <https://www.fivesolas.com/suzerain.htm>, accessed May 2021).

7 Let's talk about sex

1 'Talking with Your Teens about Sex: Going Beyond "the Talk"', Centers for Disease Control and Prevention, 21 November 2019 (available online at: <https://www.cdc.gov/healthyyouth/protective/factsheets/talking_teens.htm>, accessed May 2021).

2 Heard in a training session a number of years ago.

3 Timothy Keller, 'The Meaning of Shalom in the Bible', NIV (available online at: <https://www.thenivbible.com/blog/meaning-shalom-bible/>, accessed May 2021).

4 Inspiration taken from the ALGEE acronym used in the Mental Health First Aid Course material.

5 With thanks to Mark Arnold for kindly helping to shape this section.

6 One excellent resource is 'All Inclusive?' training by Mark Arnold, Additional Needs Ministry Director, Urban Saints. More information is available at: <https://www.urbansaints.org/allinclusive> (accessed June 2021).

7 'Reachout ASC – Lynn McCann' (available online at: <https://reachoutasc.com/resources/downloadable-resources/>, accessed May 2021).

8 The sexual health thing

1 '0–18 years: guidance for all doctors. Sexual activity', General Medical Council (available online at: <https://www.gmc-uk.org/ethical-guidance/ethical-guidance-for-doctors/0-18-years/sexual-activity>, accessed June 2021).

9 The safety thing

1 Sophie Foster, 'How many sexual partners the average person has – where do you rank?' *Daily Star*, 25 August 2020 (available online at:

<https://www.dailystar.co.uk/love-sex/how-many-sexual-partners-average-22573869>, accessed June 2021).

2 Donna Ferguson, 'How UK schoolgirls finally found voice to tell of sexual abuse', *The Guardian*, 28 March 2021 (available online at: <https://www.theguardian.com/society/2021/mar/27/how-schoolgirls-finally-found-voice-to-tell-of-sexual-abuse>, accessed May 2021).

3 Donna Ferguson, 'How UK schoolgirls finally found voice to tell of sexual abuse'.

4 Today Programme, Radio 4, March 2021.

5 Michaeljon Alexander-Scott, Emma Bell and Jenny Holden, 'DFID Guidance Notes: Shifting Social Norms to Tackle Violence Against Women and Girls (VAWG)', January 2016 (available online at: <https://assets.publishing.service.gov.uk/government/uploads/system/uploads/attachment_data/file/507845/Shifting-Social-Norms-tackle-Violence-against-Women-Girls3.pdf>, accessed May 2021).

6 Ana J. Bridges, Robert Wosnitzer, Erica Scharrer, Chyng Sun and Rachael Liberman, 'Aggression and Sexual Behavior in Best-Selling Pornography Videos: A Content Analysis Update', 26 October 2010 (available online at: <https://journals.sagepub.com/doi/10.1177/1077801210382866>, accessed May 2021).

7 Judith K. Balswick and Jack O. Balswick, *Authentic Human Sexuality: An integrated Christian approach* (Downers Grove: IVP, 1999), p. 276.

8 'Safe?' by Youthscape and Thirtyone:eight is a scenario-based safeguarding resource designed for anyone working with teenagers to help you recognize the signs of various types of abuse or safeguarding risk by creating hypothetical situations and asking you to consider your response. It is available to purchase at <https://www.youthscape.co.uk/store/product/safe> (accessed May 2021).

9 'Sexual behaviour in children', NSPCC (available online at: <https://www.nspcc.org.uk/keeping-children-safe/sex-relationships/sexual-behaviour-children/>, accessed May 2021).

10 'A new approach to keeping young people safe online' *Financial Times* partner content (available online at: <https://www.ft.com/partnercontent/everfi-2/a-new-approach-to-keeping-young-people-safe-online.html>, accessed May 2021).

11 N. T. Wright, *Paul for Everyone: The prison letters* (London: SPCK, 2002), p. 57.

10 The desire thing

1 Fyre Festival, 'Announcing Fyre Festival', YouTube, 12 January 2017 (available online at: <https://www.youtube.com/watch?v=mz5kY3RsmKo>, accessed June 2021).

2 Quoted in Bret McCabe, 'René Girard and the Mysterious Nature of Desire', John Hopkins University, 8 August 2018 (available online at: <https://hub.jhu.edu/2018/08/08/rene-girard-evolution-desire/>, accessed June 2021).

3 Sarah Coakley, *God, Sexuality and the Self: An essay 'On the Trinity'* (Cambridge: Cambridge University Press, 2013), p. 10.

4 St Augustine, *Homily on the First Letter of John*.

5 Lewis Corner, 'GAY TIMES research finds that only 36% of today's youth identify as "exclusively straight"', *Gay Times*, n.d. (available online at: <https://www.gaytimes.co.uk/life/gay-times-research-finds-that-only-36-of-todays-youth-identify-as-exclusively-straight/>, accessed June 2021).

6 Quoted in Emma Powys, 'Stonewall Founder Matthew Parris believes sexuality can be "re-channelled"', My Pink News, 5 March 2021 (available online at: <https://www.pinknews.co.uk/2021/03/05/stonewall-matthew-parris-sexuality-gender-cure-lgbt/>, accessed June 2021).

11 The intimacy thing

1 The 5 Love Languages (available online at: <www.5lovelanguages.com>, accessed May 2021).